God's Intention Concerning Christ and the Church

Witness Lee

Living Stream Ministry

Anaheim, CA • www.lsm.org

First Edition, February 2004.

ISBN 0-7363-2545-X

Published by

Living Stream Ministry
2431 W. La Palma Ave., Anaheim, CA 92801 U.S.A.
P. O. Box 2121, Anaheim, CA 92814 U.S.A.

Printed in the United States of America

04 05 06 07 08 09 10 / 9 8 7 6 5 4 3 2 1

CONTENTS

PREFACE

This book is composed of ten messages given by Brother Witness Lee in April of 1963 in a conference in San Diego, California. These messages were not reviewed by the speaker.

CHAPTER ONE

EXPERIENCING CHRIST AS OUR PORTION

Scripture Reading: Col. 1:12-19, 27; 2:9, 16-17; 3:4, 9-11; Phil. 3:7-8, 10; John 1:4; 10:10b; 11:25; 6:35, 57, 63

CHRIST BEING GIVEN TO US
TO BE OUR UNIQUE PORTION

Colossians 1:12 says, "Giving thanks to the Father, who has qualified you for a share of the allotted portion of the saints in the light." What is the portion of the saints spoken of in this verse? Since we have been qualified to partake of this portion, we should consider what it is. If we read the book of Colossians carefully, we will realize that the portion of the saints is Christ Himself. Christ is our portion, and we partake of Him. We need to be clear that in eternity past God the Father predestinated us to partake of Christ and Christ alone. It is God's intention that we would partake of nothing other than Christ Himself.

It was in keeping with this intention that Paul wrote his Epistle to the Colossians. At the time of his writing, Paul realized that many things other than Christ had come into the churches. Thus, Paul wrote this letter to the believers to reveal to them God's thought that Christ was meant to be our unique portion and that God has nothing for us other than Christ Himself.

THE CHRIST WHO IS OUR PORTION
BEING THE IMAGE AND EMBODIMENT OF GOD
AND THE CENTER OF THE UNIVERSE

If we carefully read the book of Colossians along with the rest of the Scriptures, we will see that the Christ who is our portion is everything; He is the image and embodiment of God and the center of the entire universe. Colossians 1:15 reveals that Christ is the image of the invisible God. God is invisible; no one can see Him. As the image of God, Christ is the manifestation and declaration of God, the One through whom we are able to see and know God (John 1:18). Christ is also the One in whom all the fullness of the Godhead was pleased to dwell bodily (Col. 1:19; 2:9). All that God is and has is in Christ. He is the expression and embodiment of God. Without Christ and apart from Christ, we cannot meet God, touch God, or contact God. If we desire to have God, we must have Christ, because God is in Christ, and Christ embodies God. In addition to being the image of the invisible God and the One in whom all the fullness of the Godhead dwells, Christ is the One through whom and for whom the entire universe was created (1:16). All things were made by Christ and for Christ. Christ is also the One in whom all things cohere (v. 17). He is the holding center of the entire universe. The whole universe is like a wheel, and Christ is the hub. A wheel subsists in its hub. If you take away the hub from a wheel, the wheel will simply fall apart. In the same way, if there were no Christ in this universe, everything would fall apart. Christ is the cohering power and center that holds together every human being and the entire universe. Thus, we can see that Christ is everything. To God He is the image and embodiment, and to the universe He is the center. This is the Christ who has been given to us by God to be our portion.

THE CHRIST WHO IS OUR PORTION BEING OUR LIFE

In addition to seeing God's intention that Christ would be our portion, we need to consider why God desires this. For what reason is Christ our portion? In the book of Colossians Paul reveals that Christ is our portion so that He can be our life and everything. In chapter three Paul uses the expression *Christ our life* (v. 4). We know that everything related to life is quite mysterious. No one, not even today's scientists, are able to explain what life is. After a person dies, he still has a body and appears the same as when he was alive. The only difference is that he no longer has life within him. No one can explain what life is, but we know that there is such a reality. We also know that our physical life is not the real life because our physical life is not an eternal life; it lasts for only a short time. Thus, we need the real life, which is Christ Himself. Christ is our life.

THE CHRIST WHO IS OUR PORTION BEING EVERYTHING TO US

In Colossians Paul reveals that Christ is not only our life but also our everything. Christ is all and in all (v. 11), and He is the reality of every positive thing in the universe. Paul says that food, drink, the feasts, the new moon, and the Sabbath are all shadows, the body of which is Christ (2:16-17). The shadow is not what is real; the body of the shadow is what is real. Thus, as the body of all the shadows, Christ is the reality of every positive thing in the universe. In a sense, the food we eat and the water we drink are not real. These things are merely shadows of the reality, which is simply Christ. Thus, if we do not have Christ, we are hungry and thirsty and have nothing (John 4:13-14; 7:37; 6:33, 35). Daily we are surrounded by light, but the light we see is a shadow, pointing to the One who is the real light and reminding us that we need the real light. Christ is the real light (9:5); if we do not have Him, we are in darkness (8:12). We may have many articles of clothing and may dress very well, but we must realize that our clothing is not our real covering. Our real covering and clothing are Christ Himself. We need to put on Christ; otherwise, we are naked in the eyes of God (Rom. 13:14; Gal. 3:27; Rev. 3:17; cf. Col. 3:10-11). If we do not have Christ, outwardly we may appear healthy and well-dressed, but in reality we are poor, hungry, naked, and in darkness. God's intention in making Christ our portion is that Christ would be everything to us.

Since Christ is the reality of every positive thing, and since it is God's desire that Christ would be everything to us, we need to experience Christ in every way. For example, we need to experience Christ as our clothing. I can illustrate this with an experience that some of my co-workers and I had. One time a number of us were invited to a feast. When we arrived at the feast, we noticed that everyone was dressed in a very fancy way except for us. As servants of the Lord, we did not like to dress in a worldly way, but everyone around us was dressed in such a way. At that time I had an inward feeling, and I said within myself, "All of you here think that you are dressed in a fancy way, but you must realize that my clothing is much better than yours. My clothing is much better because I am covered with Christ. While I am here among you, I am clothed with Christ, and I am expressing Christ." This was a practical experience of Christ as my clothing.

EXPERIENCING CHRIST AS EVERYTHING TO US

By Experiencing Christ in an Ordinary Way

Since Christ is our portion, we must apply Him and experience Him practically in every way. How can we do this? How can we experience Christ as everything to us? Nearly every Christian knows that Jesus said that He is the bread of life (John 6:35, 48), but how many Christians know how to experience Christ as the bread of life in a practical way? Some may say that the way to experience Christ as the bread of life is to read and study the Word. This is very close, but we need something further. Others may say that they have experienced Christ as their bread by experiencing a particular verse in the Bible. A sister once told me that several times she had experienced Psalm 23:4, which says, "Even though I walk / Through the valley of the shadow of death, / I do not fear evil, / For You are with me; / Your rod and Your staff, / They comfort me." This is good, but we need to learn to experience Christ not only in an extraordinary way but also in a very ordinary way.

Most Christians today like to hear things that sound wonderful to them. They like to hear how great the Lord is. However, most do not realize that the Lord desires us to experience Him in a very practical and ordinary way. We can see this desire in His statement in John 6:48, which says, "I am the bread of life." The day before making this statement, the Lord fed five thousand people with only a few pieces of bread and some fish. After performing this miracle, the people came to Him, thinking, "This One is so wonderful. Let us make Him king." Faced with such a situation, the Lord seemed to say to them, "I do not want to be a king. I want to be a piece of bread. I want to be the bread of life for you to take. He who eats Me shall live because of Me." The people viewed the Lord as being very great, but the Lord likened Himself to something very ordinary—bread. From this we can see that the Lord's desire is that we would experience Him in a very practical and even ordinary way in our daily living. It is precious that the Lord does wonderful things in our lives, but it is even more precious that we can experience Him in a very practical way. Day by day we can take Christ as our food and live by Him.

By Taking Christ as Our Life

We can live by Christ day by day and experience Christ as everything to us because Christ is our real life. The life that we received from our parents is not our real life; it is only a figure and a shadow, pointing us to Christ who is our real life. If we do not have Christ, we do not have life. We need to take Christ as our life and live by Him. We should no longer live by the natural life that we received from our parents but by the life that we received through regeneration, the life that is Christ Himself.

By Seeing That Christ Is the Spirit within Us

What then is the practical way for us to experience Christ as our life and everything? We surely need to receive the Lord's word, but in addition to receiving His word, we need to experience Christ Himself. In order to do this, we need to see that today Christ is the Spirit (1 Cor. 15:45b; 2 Cor. 3:17). John 6:63 tells us that it is the Spirit who gives life. Christ is our life, the Spirit gives life, and Christ today is the Spirit. Thus, the way for us to experience Christ as life is to experience the Spirit. Moreover, we need to realize that the Spirit is within us and that He is within us as life (Rom. 8:11, 2). If we want to enjoy Him as our life supply day by day, we need to remember that the Lord is already within us (v. 10; 2 Cor. 13:5). The Lord is in the heavens, but He is not only in the heavens; He is also within us. This is truly wonderful. Today Christ is the Spirit dwelling within us as our life.

By Denying Our Natural Life

The fact that Christ is dwelling within us as our life is wonderful. The problem, however, is that we have our own natural life within us as well. We have two lives within us, and the question is, By which life will we live? Will we live by our natural life or by the spiritual life that we have received, which is Christ Himself? If we desire to live by Christ, every morning we should rise up and pray, "Lord, this is a new day. Today grant me the mercy and the grace to live by You and not by myself. I realize that I have You in my spirit as my life, so I ask You to enable me to live You and to not live myself." We all must endeavor to experience Christ as our life.

To be a real and normal Christian, we must not merely learn doctrines and teachings about Christ. This is not good enough. Instead, we must realize that Christ is a living person who is now living within us. He is not a doctrine but a living person who is living in us to be our life. We need to realize this and then learn to take, apply, and appropriate Him as our life in our daily living. When we deal with our spouse, we need to take Christ as our life. When we are about to speak with others, we need to take Christ as our life. We need to realize that Christ is our life and then apply Him in all the things that happen to us in our daily living. By doing this, we will enjoy Christ as the portion of the saints.

By Counting All Things Other Than Christ to Be Loss

In Philippians 3 Paul says that he counted everything other than Christ to be loss, dross, and even refuse, dung. He tells us that he suffered the loss of all things in order to gain Christ and win Christ (vv. 7-8). We all need the same realization and experience. Everything in this universe is nothing; only Christ is reality. Even if we had the whole universe, we would have nothing, because Christ is everything. At most, everything in this universe is a shadow, pointing to our need for Christ to be everything to us. Christ is our life, our all in all, and the unique portion given to us by God. Thus, we need to experience Him in a practical way.

By Making a Decision

To experience Christ as everything to us in a practical way requires that we make a decision. Each of us needs to make a decision that from this moment on, we will learn to be a normal Christian, one who experiences Christ in a practical way. We need to make a decision that we would not simply come to the meetings, pray occasionally, read the Word from time to time, and learn some of the teachings of Christianity. We must decide that moment by moment and day by day we will endeavor to exercise to experience Christ as our life and everything in a very practical way. Even right now we need to make up our mind to be a Christian in a practical sense, not merely a Christian who learns doctrines and teachings about Christ. The normal Christian life, the real Christian life, is a life full of Christ as our life and life supply. A normal Christian is one who is always taking Christ as his life in an ordinary and practical way in his daily living. This is very simple yet very real.

By Doing Everything by Christ

Young believers often come to me and ask me why they should not do certain things. I answer them by telling them that if they can engage in a particular activity and say that Christ is the One doing it in them, it is all right for them to do it. Once a college student came to me and asked, "Brother Lee, today we are in the twentieth century. What is wrong with young people going to the movies? Why shouldn't they go?" I answered this young brother, "Brother, check with the Lord, and if you can say that you are going to the movies by Christ and not by yourself, it is okay for you to go. Can you tell the Lord, 'Lord, I am going to the movies not by myself but by You'?" A sister once came to me and said, "I know that as a wife and a mother I should never lose my temper but should be very gentle. The problem is that I easily lose my temper. What shall I do? I have prayed about this many times, asking the Lord to help me not to lose my temper, but the more I pray, the more I lose my temper." I answered this sister, saying, "Sister, there is a very practical way to deal with this situation. When you are going to lose your temper, you should tell the Lord, 'Lord, I am about to lose my temper, so I will try to lose my temper not by myself but by You. Lord, I am about to say something bad to my husband, so I will try to do so not by myself but by You.' This is very simple. If you try to do this, you will find that although it is very easy to lose your temper by yourself, once you try to lose your temper by Christ, your temper will be gone."

We should never do anything by ourselves because we are not good enough to do anything. On the other hand, Christ is good enough to do everything. We should not think that speaking with our children is an easy matter and that we do not need Christ in this matter. This is not correct. We need Christ even in such a small matter. When we are speaking with our children, we should tell the Lord, "Lord, I am here speaking to this child not by myself but by You." If we practice to speak to the Lord in this way, we will receive much blessing.

The urgent need among God's children today is the practical experience of Christ. Many believers know doctrines and teachings concerning Christ, but very few of them experience Christ in a practical way in their daily living. Thus, whenever we are going to do anything, we should exercise to say to the Lord, "Lord, I am going to do this particular thing not by myself but by You. You are my life, my life supply, and my everything." As believers, we are not dealing with a set of teachings or doctrines; we are dealing with a living person— the living Son of the living God. We are dealing with this person, and He is our life, life supply, and everything. If we exercise in this way, it will change our life. We will experience a great transformation, and we will be delivered from our self and filled with Christ. As a result, we will become the expression of Christ. God has qualified us for a share of the allotted portion of the saints in the light, and this portion is simply Christ Himself to be our life and everything that we might express Him for His glory.

CHAPTER TWO

THE NEED FOR LIFE, POWER, AND THE GROWTH IN LIFE

Scripture Reading: Rom. 8:2, 6, 9, 14-16, 26; Gal. 4:6; Luke 24:46-49; Acts 1:5, 8

THE SPIRIT BEING THE SPIRIT OF GOD, THE SPIRIT OF CHRIST, AND THE SPIRIT OF LIFE

In Romans 8:2 Paul refers to the Spirit as "the Spirit of life." Paul does not refer simply to the Spirit but to the Spirit of life. In so doing, he stresses the matter of life. In the second half of verse 6 Paul continues this emphasis when he says, "The mind set on the spirit is life and peace." Verse 9 then reveals two additional titles of the Spirit. This verse reads, "You are not in the flesh, but in the spirit, if indeed the Spirit of God dwells in you. Yet if anyone does not have the Spirit of Christ, he is not of Him." In this verse Paul calls the Spirit "the Spirit of God" and "the Spirit of Christ." Thus, in Romans 8 Paul uses three different titles when speaking of the Spirit— "the Spirit of life," "the Spirit of God," and "the Spirit of Christ." This reveals that the Spirit of God is the Spirit of Christ and that the Spirit of Christ is the Spirit of life. God is in Christ (John 14:10-11). God is the Father, Christ is the Son, and the Father and the Son are one (10:30). Not only is God in Christ, but this Christ is also life (11:25; 14:6). God is in Christ to be life to us (Col. 3:4). Moreover, God in Christ is life to us as the Spirit. This is why Paul uses these three titles in Romans 8 to speak of the Spirit. God is in Christ to be life to us as the Spirit of God, the Spirit of Christ, and the Spirit of life.

THE SPIRIT BEING THE SPIRIT OF GOD'S SON
TO MAKE US SONS OF GOD

Partaking of the Spirit through Regeneration

How are we able to have a share in this Spirit? Romans 8:14 tells us the answer: "For as many as are led by the Spirit of God, these are sons of God." This indicates that we have a share in the Spirit by means of our regeneration, our rebirth, which has made us sons of God. Because we have been regenerated to be the sons of God, we have a share in the Spirit of God. Verse 15 continues, "You have not received a spirit of slavery bringing you into fear again, but you have received a spirit of sonship in which we cry, Abba, Father!" The reason we cry "Abba, Father" is that we have received a spirit of sonship. This corresponds with Galatians 4:6, which says, "Because you are sons, God has sent forth the Spirit of His Son into our hearts, crying, Abba, Father!" This verse begins with, "Because you are sons...." We were made sons by regeneration. God regenerated us with His Spirit (John 3:6), and we thus became sons of God. Because we are sons, God has sent forth the Spirit of His Son into our hearts, and we cry out to God as our Father.

Galatians 4:6 reveals a fourth title of the Spirit—"the Spirit of His [God's] Son." The Spirit is the Spirit of God, the Spirit of Christ, the Spirit of life, and the Spirit of God's Son. The Spirit of God's Son corresponds to the spirit of sonship in Romans 8:15. God is in Christ, Christ is life to us, and this causes us to become sons of God. A son always has the life of his father. If you do not have your father's life, you are not your father's son. The relationship between a son and a father is one of life. In like manner, we are the sons of God because we have received the life of God through regeneration. Through whom did we receive the life of God? We received the life of God through the Spirit of God as the Spirit of the Son, who is the Spirit of life. It is the Spirit who brought the life of God into us. The Spirit is the reality of the life of God (John 16:13). In fact, He Himself is the life of God (11:25). This is why He is referred to as the Spirit of life. Without the Spirit, there is no life. The divine life of God is in the Spirit, and the

Spirit is the very essence and element of the divine life. Thus, if you have the Spirit, you have the divine life, and if you have the divine life, you are a son of God.

How do we know that we have the Spirit of God within us? Romans 8:16 tells us the answer: "The Spirit Himself witnesses with our spirit that we are children of God." We know that we have the Spirit within us because the Spirit witnesses with our spirit that we are children of God. Whenever we have the feeling that we are children of God, we must realize that this feeling is something of the Spirit. It may be very weak, but this little feeling is strong proof that we are indeed children of God and that we have the Spirit of God within us. Although we may be sinful, worldly, and weak, and although we may fall and commit sins against God, we still have the feeling within that we are children of God, and we still automatically and spontaneously call out to God, saying, "O Father, my heavenly Father." This is proof that we have the Spirit of the Son witnessing in our spirit, which is the innermost and deepest part of our being. Even after we sin against God, we still sense in the innermost and deepest part of our being that we are children of God. We may feel sorrowful and ashamed of what we have done, yet we still sense in our deepest part that we are children of God. This proves that we have the spirit of sonship, which is the Spirit of God's Son, the Spirit of life, the Spirit of Christ, and the Spirit of God.

Being a Son Being a Matter of Life, Not of Power

As long as a child has the life of his father, he is his father's son. No matter how weak the child is, he is his father's son. On the other hand, if a child does not have the life of a certain man, he cannot be that man's genuine son, regardless of how strong he is. Being a son is not a matter of power; being a son is a matter of life. A baby may be only one and a half feet long and weigh only six pounds, yet that baby is still his father's son because he has his father's life. That baby may be childish and powerless, and he may not have any gifts or even be able to see, speak, walk, or eat properly. Nevertheless, he is the son of his father because he has his father's life. This point is illustrated in Romans 8:26, which says,

"Moreover, in like manner the Spirit also joins in to help us
in our weakness, for we do not know for what we should pray
as is fitting, but the Spirit Himself intercedes for us with
groanings which cannot be uttered." This verse reveals how
weak we are at times. Sometimes we are so weak that we do
not even know how to pray. We are like babies. Babies do not
know how to ask for anything and are very weak. Thus, their
mothers must know what they need and intercede for them.
The Spirit is like a mother within us, interceding for us all
the time with groanings which cannot be uttered. Because of
our childishness, we are unable to utter what we need. A baby
cannot utter what he needs, but his mother, who is outside of
him, can utter what she feels her baby needs. This is similar
to our situation, but in our situation our "mother," the Spirit,
is inside of us. The Spirit within us utters for us what we
need. Often we have a burden to pray, but we do not know how
to utter our burden. Therefore, we can only groan. Although
we may not be able to give utterance to our burden, we should
be assured that whenever we have the burden to groan from
the deepest part of our being, the Spirit is working within us.
Often we face situations in which we do not know what to do
or how to pray, but we have the burden to go to the Father,
to go to the Lord, and to groan. When we have this kind of
experience, the Spirit of God, who is the Spirit of the Son, the
Spirit of life, is working within us. Although we may be weak,
we can be assured that we have the Spirit of life within us. As
long as we have the Spirit of life, the life of God, within us, we
are sons of God no matter how weak we may be. Thus, it is
wrong to say that one who does not have power is not a son of
God. Being a son of God is a matter of life, that is, of the Spirit
of life.

NEEDING POWER TO CARRY OUT THE LORD'S WORK

Now that we have seen that being a son of God is a matter
of life, we must also see that in order to carry out the Lord's
work, we need power. In Luke 24:46-48 the Lord said to the
disciples, "Thus it is written, that the Christ would suffer and
rise up from the dead on the third day, and that repentance
for forgiveness of sins would be proclaimed in His name to all

the nations, beginning from Jerusalem. You are witnesses of these things." In these verses the Lord referred to the disciples as witnesses. When the Lord spoke these words to the disciples, they had undoubtedly already received the Spirit of life (John 20:22). As a result, they were clearly children of God. The Lord's words in Luke 24:46-48 reveal that they were also witnesses of the risen Lord. Receiving the Spirit of life had made them both children of God and witnesses. Nevertheless, in verse 49 the Lord said, "Behold, I send forth the promise of My Father upon you; but as for you, stay in the city until you put on power from on high." The phrase *the promise of My Father* in this verse refers to the Spirit of power (Joel 2:28-29), and the phrase *put on power from on high* can also be translated "be clothed with power from on high" (Luke 24:49, ASV). Although the disciples had received the Spirit of life to become sons of God and witnesses of the risen Lord, they needed something more; they needed to be clothed, covered, and equipped with the Spirit of power. Even a little baby needs to be clothed. If you leave your baby at home, he may not need to be clothed, but it would be a shame to bring your baby into public naked. Even though that baby has your life, he also needs to be clothed. In like manner, although we have received the life of God and have the Spirit of life within us, making us sons of God, we also need to be clothed with the Spirit of power from on high. Clearly, Peter, John, and James had received the Spirit of life prior to the day of Pentecost (John 20:22). However, although they had received the Spirit of life, they needed something more; they needed to be clothed and equipped with the Spirit of power so that they could stand up to serve the Lord and preach the gospel. They needed the Spirit of power from on high as their equipment. This is why the Lord told them to stay in Jerusalem until they were clothed with power from on high.

Acts 1:5 says, "John baptized with water, but you shall be baptized in the Holy Spirit not many days from now." The baptism in the Holy Spirit was accomplished on the day of Pentecost. Verse 8 begins with, "You shall receive power when the Holy Spirit comes upon you." This verse does not say, "You shall receive life when the Holy Spirit comes into you." Rather, it indicates that the Holy Spirit would come upon the disciples and that they would receive power. The verse continues, saying, "You shall be My witnesses both in Jerusalem and in all Judea and Samaria and unto the uttermost part of the earth." All of this happened on the day of Pentecost. On the day of Pentecost the disciples received the baptism of the Holy Spirit, and this baptism was not a matter of life but of power. When we initially accept the Lord Jesus as our personal Savior, we receive the Spirit into us as the Spirit of life. However, in addition to receiving the Spirit of life into us, we also need the Spirit as the Spirit of power to come upon us to equip us and clothe us. Only then will we be equipped to minister and to serve the Lord.

NEEDING THE GROWTH IN LIFE
TO PROPERLY USE THE POWER WE RECEIVE

In addition to receiving the Spirit of life, we must receive the Spirit of power. However, in order to properly handle the power that we receive by being clothed with the Spirit, we must have the adequate growth in life. A baby has life, but if you clothe him with very nice clothing, he may misuse his clothing because he does not have the adequate growth in life. Since he lacks maturity, he may spoil his new clothes. This is the case with many of the Lord's children. Many have genuinely received the baptism and power of the Spirit, but they do not know how to use it, and in many cases they misuse it. This is because although they have the life of God, they do not have the growth in life.

This was the condition of the believers in Corinth. The believers in Corinth had received the baptism of the Holy Spirit and the gifts that accompany this baptism. Thus, in 1 Corinthians 1:7 the apostle Paul told them that they did not lack in any gift. They had all the gifts, including the gifts of speaking in tongues, prophesying, and healing. However, in 3:1 the apostle told them that they were infants in Christ, and in chapters twelve through fourteen he instructed them regarding how to properly use the gifts. Because they did not have the adequate growth in life, they misused the gifts and damaged the church. Thus, Paul had to instruct them concerning the proper way to deal with the gifts.

In chapter thirteen Paul told the Corinthians that the best way to deal with the gifts is love. Love is the most excellent way. What then is love? Love is something of life. Galatians 5 reveals that when we are mature in the life of the Spirit, we have love. The Spirit is the Spirit of life, and the first of the nine items of the fruit of the Spirit listed in verses 22 and 23 is love. After I initially received the Lord, I was genuinely saved, but I was still a babe. Thus, I could not tolerate anyone who was not like me. I was brought up among believers who emphasized the teachings in the Scriptures very much. I was exposed to the teachings of Pember, Panton, Darby, and Newton, and I heard numerous messages concerning the seventy weeks in Daniel, the tribulation and the rapture, and the prophecies related to Israel, the church, and the Gentiles. If anyone held different views than I did concerning these teachings, I could not tolerate him. I could not love anyone who was different from me. However, today although I am not yet fully mature, I am able to love all kinds of Christians. If you are unable to love others, this proves that you are not mature in life. If you are mature, you will simply love everyone. In addition, you will consider others when you exercise your gifts. You may have a certain gift, but you will ask yourself, "If I use my gift, will it benefit others?" If it will not, you will not use it. This is love, which is the issue of maturity in life. Love is the most excellent way for us to exercise our gifts.

In 1 Corinthians the Corinthian believers lacked the growth in life, so in 2 Corinthians Paul stressed the growth in life and did not mention the gifts. He told the Corinthians that although their outer man was decaying, their inner man was being renewed day by day (4:16). In doing so, he referred to the growth of their spiritual life. The fact that Paul did not mention the gifts in 2 Corinthians does not mean that there is no need for the gifts. There is still a need for the gifts, but there is also a need for something more—the growth in life, which enables us to use the gifts properly.

To be proper Christians we need three things—life, power, and the growth in life. With this light we can examine the present situation in Christianity today. On the one hand, some of the Lord's children have the divine life and a measure of growth in life, but they do not have any power. They lack the equipment and the power of release. They do not know the gift of Pentecost and may even oppose this matter. In this regard they are not correct. To oppose this is absolutely wrong. On the other hand, some of the Lord's children have received the power of the baptism of the Spirit and the gifts, but regrettably, they do not have the growth in life. They are still young in the divine life; hence, they do many unseemly things, things that are not decent, not good for the glory of God, and not good for the edification of others or even for themselves. They may even misuse the gifts to the extent that they damage themselves. Many who have experienced the baptism of the Spirit are unable to go on in the divine life. They simply remain as babes and are childish, not knowing how to grow in life. However, there are at least a few Christians who have the divine life, the baptism of the Spirit, and also the growth in life. These ones are equipped and qualified to properly minister to others and to themselves. They have life, power, and growth. The clear revelation in the Word is that we need all three. We all should pray that the Lord's children would be adjusted. Those who call themselves "fundamental" need power; they need the experience of the baptism of the Holy Spirit. Those who have the experience of the baptism of the Holy Spirit still need to grow in life. With life, power, and growth, all the dear children of the Lord will be a profit to the building up of the Body of Christ.

Some who call themselves fundamentalists oppose the experience of the baptism of the Spirit. Some even say that the baptism of the Spirit is something of the devil. This is not right. All God's children should be for this, not against this. Thus, we need to pray much that the Lord would vindicate this matter and prove to these dear ones that this is something of Him. Of course, it is true that some believers who are still childish have misused the baptism of the Spirit and have gone to the extreme. In 1935 when I was in China, we realized that the baptism of the Spirit was something of the Lord, so we encouraged the saints to seek and to take this experience.

By doing this, we opened the door for this experience. However, when some of the brothers and sisters received this experience, they took it to an extreme and began to do many strange things. In one meeting a brother began to act like the donkey that had carried the Lord into Jerusalem. As he did so, some of the other brothers and sisters took off their sweaters and coats and laid them on the ground in front of the brother. Another sister began to prophesy when she received the baptism of the Spirit. She prophesied that a sister who had died of tuberculosis would come back to life. She told the other saints not to get a coffin because the sister who had died would rise up at twelve o'clock the next day. This prevented the family from taking any action. However, when the next day arrived, nothing happened. Eventually, one of the elders had to come and tell the family, "By the authority of the Lord, I tell you that you must bury this sister." No one can deny that there is a need for some balance. This is why, along with the experience of the baptism of the Spirit, we also need the growth in life. Nevertheless, although some have taken the baptism of the Spirit to an extreme, this does not mean that it is of the devil. Rather, it is something of the Lord, and we need to seek it and experience it.

The Spirit today is both the Spirit of life and the Spirit of power. By receiving the Spirit of life through regeneration we are born of God to be genuine sons of God, possessing His very life. Once we have received the Spirit of life, we are genuine children of God. However, in order to carry out the Lord's work, we also need to receive the Spirit of power. By the Spirit of power we can work with the Lord for the accomplishment of His purpose. We need the Spirit of life in order to be sons, and we need the Spirit of power in order to do the Lord's work. Then, in addition to life and power, we need the growth in life. If we have life, power, and growth, we will be proper, balanced Christians who can be used by the Lord for His Body.

CHAPTER THREE

GOD'S INTENTION TO WORK CHRIST INTO US THROUGH THE CROSS AND BY THE SPIRIT

Scripture Reading: Gal. 1:16; 2:20; 3:27; 4:19; 5:4; 4:6; 3:3; 5:16, 18, 22, 25; 6:14-15

MAN'S THOUGHT VERSUS GOD'S THOUGHT

People have many different opinions concerning Christianity and religion. Most people, however, believe that the goal of Christianity is to help people do good. This thought is held both in the East and in the West and has existed in the past as well as in the present. People think that to be a Christian is to be one who tries his best to do good. We may also have this thought. The source of this thought is the tree of the knowledge of good and evil. When Adam, the father of the human race, partook of that tree, the knowledge of good and evil entered into the human race. From that time, human beings have always had the thought that they should try to do good. This thought, however, is absolutely contrary to God's thought.

In the garden of Eden there were many trees, but among these trees were two main trees—the tree of life and the tree of the knowledge of good and evil (Gen. 2:9). These two trees oppose each other. The tree of life represents God's thought, which is that man would take God in Christ as life. Christ Himself is the tree of life (John 14:6; 15:1), and God desires that we would take Christ to be our life (Col. 3:4). Adam, however, did not take in the tree of life; he took in the tree of the knowledge of good and evil (Gen. 3:6). From the time that he did this, the notion of trying to do good has been in the human race. Human beings think that trying to do good and teaching others to do good is a good thing. Every religion, including today's Christianity, has this concept, but this thought is not God's thought.

The Jews received the law from God. The law is related to knowing what is good and what is evil and trying to do good and rejecting evil. When the Jews received the law, they believed that the law was something of God's original thought (Exo. 24:3, 7). This, however, was not the case. The law was something additional; it was not something of God's original thought. For what purpose was the law added? It was added to prove that we are unable to do good and to show that even if we are able to do some good, our good does not please God (Gal. 3:19; Rom. 5:20a). The law testifies and proves that we are sinners (v. 20b; 7:7). Due to the fall of man, human beings have the knowledge of good and evil and have the thought that they should try to do good. Thus, when they learn about the law of God, they say, "This is it. This is what we should do. We should try our best to do good in order to please God." However, this is not the purpose of the law nor is it God's desire.

God's desire is to enter into us and to be mingled with us in Christ. God's intention is to work Christ into us. Christ is the manifestation of God, the embodiment of God, even God Himself (John 1:18; 1 Tim. 3:16; Col. 2:9; John 1:1, 14). The human thought is that we must try our best to do good; God's thought is that we need Christ to be wrought into us.

Some may say that they have already heard this and already know this. The question, however, is not whether we have heard this but whether we practice it. You may know this as a Christian teaching, but do you practice this in your daily life? I have discovered that the vast majority of seeking Christians still have the thought that they need to try their best to do good to please God. If you are not seeking God, you will not care about doing good to please God, but once you are revived and brought back to God, you will immediately have the thought that you must begin to try to do good to please God. You may even pray to the Lord, "Lord, in the past I have done many things against You. Now I praise You and thank You that You have brought me back to You. I know that from now on I should do good to please You. However, I know that I am weak, so I pray that You would help me." I believe that many of us have prayed in this way after being revived and brought back to the Lord. We must realize, however, that this prayer is not according to the mind and thought of God and that this kind of prayer has never been answered.

I would like to tell you a true story about a brother whom I know. When this brother was far away from God, he did not care how he behaved, but when he was brought back to the Lord, he confessed to the Lord that he had been mean to his wife and had frequently lost his temper. He confessed this to the Lord and made a decision that from that moment on he would never lose his temper again. Realizing that he had a weakness related to his temper, he prayed to the Lord, saying, "Lord, You know how weak I am. Since I am weak, I trust in You, and I ask You to help me." However, after making this decision and praying in this way, he still continued to fail. During this time he came to me and said, "Brother Lee, the more I pray that I would not lose my temper, the more I lose it, and when I pray for the Lord to help me, He does not come in and answer my prayer. What is the reason for this? In so many other situations I have prayed and have received clear evidence that the Lord has heard my prayers. Why then does it seem that when I pray regarding this matter, the Lord does not answer my prayer?" I answered this brother: "The Lord will never answer this prayer, because this prayer is not according to the mind of God." He was puzzled by this answer and replied, "What do you mean? The Bible tells us that husbands must love their wives. In light of this I realized that it was wrong for me to lose my temper with my wife and decided that I must try to be nice to my wife. How can this be contrary to the mind of God? Are you saying that I should hate my wife? Surely, that cannot be according to the mind of God." I then answered him, "I am not telling you to try to be nice to your wife or to hate your wife. Neither of these is correct. To hate your wife is according to the tree of the knowledge of good and evil, but to try to love your wife is also according to this tree. To do evil is according to the tree of the knowledge of good and evil, but to try to do good is also according to this tree. This tree is not only the tree of evil but also the tree of good." Then I asked this brother, "Brother, do you think that God's desire is to build you up to be a good man? Do you think that God's desire is to build good into you so that you will love your wife more than any other husband loves his wife? If you think this, you are wrong. God's desire is to build Christ into you and to build up Christ within you. Then, when you love your wife, it will not be you loving your wife but Christ. You must give up trying to be good and come to the Lord and say, 'Lord, I know that Your will is not that I would do good. Your will is that I would live not by myself but by You. Thus, I take You as my life.'" Then this brother asked me, "How shall I relate to my wife? Shall I continue to lose my temper all the time?" I answered him, "Brother, what you need to do is to give up the tree of the knowledge of good and evil. In other words, you must give up yourself. Forget about yourself, forget about your temper, and forget about trying to be patient with your wife. Instead, take Christ as your life. Day by day and moment by moment take Christ as your life and experience Christ as your life. Forget about your wife, forget about your patience, forget about your temper, and forget about good and evil. Forget about everything and focus on Christ alone. Simply take Christ as your life."

We should not think that only evil is versus life. Good is also versus life. Good and evil are both on the tree that is in opposition to the tree of life. Hatred is not life, and natural human love also is not life. Being proud is not life, and being humble is not life. Losing one's temper is not life, and being patient is not life. Neither evil nor good is life. What then is life? Life is Christ, and Christ is life (John 11:25; 14:6). Our evil and our good, our hatred and our love, and our pride and our humility are all opposed to life. Only Christ is life.

We must also be clear that God has no desire to build us up to be good. God's thought is that Christ would be built up within us. God wants to build something other than evil and good into us; God wants to build Christ as life into us. He wants to build into us not love but Christ, not humility but Christ, not a good temper but Christ, and not patience but Christ. To be a normal Christian is not to be one who tries to do good;

neither is it to be one who does evil. To be a normal Christian is to be one who lives by Christ. It is not easy for us to forget about trying to do something, but we must realize that to be a Christian simply means to be one who lives Christ and takes Christ as the tree of life. Christ is the living One. He is the Spirit and the life within us (2 Cor. 3:17; Col. 3:4). As such, He is real, and we can experience Him in a very real way. We simply need to take Him as our life moment by moment. This is God's thought and God's desire.

OUR PROGRESSIVE EXPERIENCE
OF HAVING CHRIST WORKED INTO OUR BEING

Christ Being Revealed in Us

Our experience of Christ being worked into our being is progressive and involves several steps. At the very moment we received Christ as our Savior, Christ entered into us. We may not have known that Christ had entered into us, but this is what happened, and this was our experience. This is the first step that God takes in His plan to work Christ into us; that is, He enters into us and reveals Christ within us.

This matches the experience of the apostle Paul. Before he was saved, Paul was a very religious person (Gal. 1:13-14; Phil. 3:4-6). He spent all his time trying to do good. Then one day the Lord opened his eyes. In Galatians Paul declared that one day it pleased God to reveal Christ in him (1:15-16). At that moment Paul realized that he had been wrong. He realized that to be a religious person and to try to do good was wrong. Thus, he was adjusted, and his thinking changed. From that time on, the apostle Paul simply forgot about everything other than Christ and counted everything that had been gain to him as loss on account of Christ (Phil. 3:7). Formerly, he had thought that religion was the best thing, but when Christ was revealed in him, he realized that religion was a loss. As a result, he gave up all his good works and religious activities for Christ.

Although I was saved when I was very young, I was not taught properly in Christianity. No one ever told me in a clear way that Christ had entered into me. The denomination that

I was raised in did not have such a teaching. Nevertheless, through my own times of prayer with the Lord, I eventually received the thought and the feeling that Christ was in me. The more I prayed, the more I had the sense within that Christ was in me. I had been taught that the Lord was far above us in the third heavens. Thus, my original thought when I began to pray to the Lord was that He was far away from me. However, as I began to spend time with the Lord in prayer, I began to sense that the Lord was very close to me, even within me. I had the strong sense that the Lord was within me, especially when I encountered difficulties and trials. As believers, we all must realize that Christ is in us (2 Cor. 13:5).

Putting On Christ

In addition to having Christ revealed in us, the apostle Paul tells us that we have put on Christ. In Galatians 3:27 he writes, "For as many of you as were baptized into Christ have put on Christ." On the one hand, Christ has been revealed in us; on the other hand, we have put on Christ. Just as we put on our clothing and are in our clothing, so also we have put on Christ and are in Christ. Thus, Christ is in us, and we are in Christ.

Christ Living in Us

In addition, Paul tells us that we must allow Christ to live in us. In Galatians 2:20 he writes, "I am crucified with Christ; and it is no longer I who live, but it is Christ who lives in me." Many of us may have the knowledge that Christ lives in us, but we still may not practice this. We must put what we know into practice every day. We must ask ourselves, "Am I living, or is Christ living in me?" This is not a doctrine. We need to exercise ourselves to live not by ourselves but by Christ.

Christ Being Formed in Us

In Galatians 4:19 Paul goes on to say that we also need Christ to be formed in us. He writes, "My children, with whom I travail again in birth until Christ is formed in you." What does it mean for Christ to be formed in us? It simply means that Christ occupies our whole being, including our heart, mind, emotion, and will. When we have the element of Christ in our thoughts, desires, and choices, we will have the form of Christ within us. Our thoughts, desires, and choices will be according to the form of Christ. As a result, we will be the image of Christ, His expression. By our being mingled with Christ in this way, Christ becomes our life and we become His expression.

Being Filled with Christ

When Christ has been revealed in us, when we have put on Christ, when Christ is living in us, and when Christ has been formed in us, we will be filled with Christ (Eph. 3:19b). To be filled with Christ is to have our entire being saturated with Christ and occupied by Christ so that when we think, Christ thinks in us; when we love, Christ loves through us; and when we make a decision, Christ makes that decision in us. Eventually, we will be mingled with Christ to such an extent that it will be difficult to discern what is of us and what is of Christ (Phil. 1:21a).

Our being mingled with Christ can be likened to water being mingled with tea. A cup of tea contains water and tea that have been mingled together. Thus, wherever there is a drop of water, there is tea. The tea is inside the water and is mingled with the water. This is similar to our relationship with Christ. We are like a cup of water, and Christ is like tea. Just as the tea is mingled with the water, so also Christ is mingled with us to be one with us. This is God's thought and desire. God's desire is not that we would do good. Rather, His desire is that we would be mingled with Christ so that Christ would be the One doing good through us. Christ is revealed in us, we put on Christ, and Christ lives in us, is formed in us, and fills us. This is the progressive way in which God works Christ into our being.

GOD WORKING CHRIST INTO US
THROUGH THE CROSS AND BY THE SPIRIT

Applying the Cross in Our Daily Life

The book of Galatians reveals that God's desire that Christ would be worked into our being is accomplished by two means—the cross and the Spirit. Several times in Galatians the apostle Paul tells us that we have been crucified with Christ (2:20; 6:14). Since we have been crucified, we are dead to the world, the flesh, and everything other than Christ. Since we are dead, we must learn to apply the cross in our daily life. Christ is living within us. Thus, whenever we are going to do something, we must remember that we have been crucified with Christ and ask ourselves, "Am I doing this, or is Christ doing this?" This is to check ourselves with the cross. Applying the cross in our daily life gives the Lord the ground to work Christ into our being.

Walking by the Spirit
by Following the Inner Sense

On the one hand, we need to apply the cross in our daily life. On the other hand, we need to realize that today Christ is the Spirit who is within us (1 Cor. 15:45b; 2 Cor. 3:17; cf. Rom. 8:10-11). This Spirit is always acting, moving, working, and living within us, and as a result, we always have some kind of registration, consciousness, or sense within. By this sense we can know the work of the Spirit within. As regenerated believers, we have a consciousness deep within in our inner-most part. Wherever we go and whatever we do, we always have this consciousness within us. If we are about to do something that is not of God, we are conscious that we do not have peace within, and if we are about to do something that is of God, we have a sense of peace within. This peace is a kind of registration or consciousness that we can sense and feel. If we desire to walk according to the Spirit, we must follow this consciousness within us. God has given us His Spirit (Acts 2:38; Rom. 5:5; 2 Cor. 5:5; 1 John 4:13), and this very Spirit is living within us as the Spirit of God's Son and the Spirit of life (Gal. 4:6; Rom. 8:2). Thus, we must walk according to Him and live by Him (Gal. 5:16, 25). The secret to this is simply to act according to our inner feeling, our inner consciousness. To walk according to the Spirit simply means to go along with this inner consciousness.

Many times after I have been speaking with a brother or sister for a while, I have the sense deep within that I should not speak anymore. No one tells me this outwardly, and there is no verse in the Scriptures that says that I should speak only for a certain amount of time or only about certain topics. Nevertheless, I often have this sense deep within that I should not continue speaking with this brother or sister. This is an example of the working of the Spirit.

We can know the working of the Spirit by this deep inner sense. If the inner feeling allows us to continue what we are doing, we may continue, but if the inner feeling does not allow it, we should stop. If we follow this inner sense, we will be the most spiritual people in the world. We will grow in life day by day, Christ will be formed within us, and we will learn a great deal concerning Christ and concerning how to cooperate with Him, how to experience Him as our life, and how to take Him as life. In addition, if we simply follow this inner sense all the time and in every matter, we will be people who please God.

This is very simple, yet many times when the Holy Spirit gives us the feeling that we should not do a particular thing, we tell Him, "Lord, let me do this thing just one more time. Next time I will not do it." As a result, the Spirit within us is often grieved (Eph. 4:30). We are constantly cheating the Lord by always doing what we want.

We may be those who come to the meetings and who sometimes even minister to the saints. Thus, outwardly, it may seem that we are good people and that there is nothing wrong with us. Apparently, we never do anything sinful. However, we know our real condition. We often break the living fellowship between the Spirit and us. We break our fellowship and communion with the Spirit. We know this, and those who are experienced in spiritual matters know this. They realize that although we appear to be good people, in actuality we have broken the living fellowship and communion with the Spirit.

If we go back to the New Testament, we will realize that the apostle Paul stressed the matter of life because he realized that without the divine life there is no Christian life. Everything related to a Christian depends upon the foundation of life. Without this we have nothing. We need to know the inner life, live by Christ, walk in the Spirit, and follow the inner consciousness moment by moment in every situation (Acts 16:6-7;

2 Cor. 2:12-13). If we do this, Christ will be able to occupy our whole being and be formed in us.

At the beginning of Galatians, Paul tells us that Christ is in us, and toward the end of the book he writes concerning the fruit of the Spirit (1:15-16; 5:22). God's first step is to send the Spirit into our hearts (4:6); His last step is to cause the Spirit to come out of us to be expressed as the items of the fruit of the Spirit. The Spirit comes into us as the Spirit of life. Thus, we must follow the Spirit and walk according to the Spirit. If we do this, then all the items of the fruit of the Spirit will come out of us as a sign and proof that we have matured in the life of the Spirit. When we reach the point when we are mature in the life of the Spirit, Christ will be formed in us and will be expressed through us. Christ will be manifested through us as all the items of the fruit of the Spirit. This is the normal Christian life.

THE NORMAL CHRISTIAN LIFE BEING COMPOSED OF THREE ITEMS— CHRIST, THE CROSS, AND THE SPIRIT

The normal Christian life is composed of three items— Christ, the cross, and the Spirit. God's intention is to work Christ into us, and He does this by the cross and by the Spirit. Through the cross we have been crucified with Christ and are dead to the world, the law, and our self (6:14; 2:19-20). We are even dead to good. We are dead to everything other than Christ. In addition to being crucified with Christ, we have also received the Holy Spirit. The Spirit is living, moving, working, and acting within us and is continually giving us an inner registration or sense. If we follow this inner sense day by day in our daily life, we will give the Spirit the full place and the full ground to saturate every part of our inner being with Christ. Then we will be filled with Christ, Christ will be formed within us, and we will have all the items of the fruit of the Spirit, by which Christ will be manifested through us. This is the normal Christian life.

I look to the Lord that we would all pay full attention to the matter of life. We need to know Christ as our life in a very practical way in our daily life. We need to experience Him as our life supply and take Him as life through the cross and by the Spirit. We must learn how to apply the cross to our being and how to follow the inner consciousness of the Spirit in order to walk by the Spirit. By our doing these things, Christ will occupy our whole being, will be formed within us, and will be manifested through us. This is God's thought and God's desire. May we all look to the Lord that this would be accomplished in and among us.

CHAPTER FOUR

A PROPER CHURCH NEEDING
TO BE FILLED WITH LIFE
AND TO BE INCLUSIVE

THE REALITY OF THE CHURCH
BEING CHRIST AS LIFE

The church is not an organization but an organism, a body—the Body of Christ (Eph. 1:22-23; Col. 1:18). As such, the church has the divine life. Although the church has the divine life, the life of the church must be healthy. For example, it is not enough for our physical body to simply have life. Many people have life in their body, but their body has lost its health and is sick. In addition to having life in our body, we need the life in our body to be healthy. Our physical body is a picture of the church, the Body of Christ. The way for the life of the church to be healthy is for the church to be filled with the experience of Christ as life. Without the experience of the life of Christ, the church has no health or reality. The reality of the church is the life of Christ; the life of the church is Christ as life (Col. 3:4).

We can never overstress the fact that the reality of the church is Christ Himself as life to every member of the Body. However, if we study the situation of Christianity, we will find that although this truth is so critical, it has been almost entirely ignored. I have studied church history and have read a number of biographies of believers from the past centuries. In addition, I was born among Christians and was brought up and educated in Christianity. I have learned much concerning the Scriptures from other Christians, and I have visited Christians in China and in many countries outside of China. Through all of this I have discovered that it is very difficult to find anyone ministering on the matter of Christ being life to us. In many places you will find groups of Christians who meet on the Lord's Day, and among these Christians there will be some who minister the Word and give messages. However, although one may be able to hear many messages, it would be very difficult to find one message on the subject of Christ as life. There would likely be a great amount of teaching, doctrine, and knowledge but very little concerning knowing Christ as life in a practical way.

If you visit the churches in the fundamentalist movement, you will discover that they are for the most part fundamental in knowledge but not in life. If they were fundamental in life, they would be more living. With life there is always an impact. This is true with all forms of life. The Lord said in John 12:24 that when a grain of wheat falls into the ground and dies, it grows up and bears much fruit. Fruit-bearing is the impact of life. However, if you visit the fundamentalist churches in the United States, there is for the most part no fruit and no impact. From this we can conclude that these churches are fundamental in their teachings but not in the experience of life.

Many dear believers in the United States have the Scofield Reference Bible in their hands. I am not against the use of this Bible. In fact, when I was young I took a correspondence course with the Moody Bible Institute that used the Scofield Reference Bible, and I received much help from it. This Bible has greatly helped some to know the Scriptures. However, for most of them this knowledge has not resulted in the real experience of Christ in their daily life. They have used this Bible to acquire knowledge with their minds, but they have remained on the line of knowledge. As a result, most of the believers in this country are very weak.

Whereas the believers in the fundamental churches are focused on knowledge, those in the Pentecostal movement are preoccupied with something other than knowledge. They are focused on power and release, but these things are not life. Thus, their experience of life is also very limited. Their mistake is that they confuse power with life.

We should never neglect the history of Christianity because this history contains the facts. We need to study this history and observe the present situation in an objective way. We should not be too subjective in studying and observing the present situation. If we visit the Assemblies of God or other branches of the Pentecostal movement, we will realize that although they have much release, they have very little life. They have much power but very little reality of Christ as life. We need to face this fact.

THE PROPER CHURCH GOVERNMENT ISSUING FROM THE GROWTH IN LIFE

The Proper Church Government Being a Matter of Life and Not Organization

The proper government of the church is the outworking of the inner life within the believers. However, since there is a lack of life among the Lord's children, it is very difficult for the proper government in the church to exist. Without life, the government of the church becomes a matter of organization. The human body is a composition of bones and tissue, and a table is a composition of a variety of parts. The difference between these two is that the human body has life and a table does not. Since a table has no life, it is a composition based solely on organization. However, since the human body has life, the bones and tissues in the body form not an organization but an organism, a composition of life. If the church does not have enough life, the government of the church will become solely a matter of organization. Someone may be able to set up a very good system for governing the church, and this system may even seem to be very scriptural. However, if the church does not have the adequate amount of life, this system will still be only an organization. A living body and a corpse are the same in terms of their parts; both have ears, a nose, bones, and legs. The difference between them is that a living body has life and a corpse does not. The proper government of the church is not a government based on organization but a government based on life.

The Proper Church Government Requiring Life Plus a Little Power

Some may think that the government of the church is

primarily a matter of power. This is not the case. Genuine church government depends eighty percent on life and only twenty percent on power. We can liken this to the government within a family. Every family must have some form of government. If a family has no government, that family will be a mess. The first thing needed for the government of a family is that the family members have life and that their life be proper and healthy. If all the members of a family were insane, they would not be able to have a proper family government. This would also be true if all the members of a family were underage. If both the children and the parents lacked the maturity in life, it would be impossible for them to have a proper family government. This demonstrates that life, that is, a proper and healthy life, is the primary necessity for government.

Once we have life, we need some power for the proper governing of the church. In order to govern we need governing power, governing knowledge, and serving ability. I have observed that in some families in the West, the parents serve food to their children during their meals. If you can serve well, you will be able to govern well. Without serving, you cannot rule. If you are to govern a church, you must serve it well. In fact, the only way to govern is by serving (Matt. 20:25-28). If you do not serve the saints, you will not be able to govern them well.

Thus, with both a family and the church, a sound government depends eighty percent on life and twenty percent on governing power, governing knowledge, and serving ability. If there are some in a local church who have the maturity in life, that church will have a good government. If all the members of a family are healthy and proper in terms of life, that family will have a proper government. In addition to having life, the family also needs a little governing power and serving ability. If a family or a local church has both life and power, the government of that family or church will be wonderful.

Stressing the Matter of Life and the Growth in Life in the Establishing of Church Government

For a proper government to be established in a local church, the primary need of the saints in that locality is life. Thus, when we were in China and were visiting a locality, the first matter we dealt with was the matter of life. In many places we did not touch the matter of church government for as long as two to three years because the saints in those places were spiritually too young. Because they were childish, it was not possible for us to set up a government among them. If we try to set up a government among the saints when they are too young, all we will be able to do is to organize them. However, if we allow the saints to mature in life, then after they have matured to a certain extent, they will develop into an organism. Then we will need to do only a small amount of appointing and arranging, and a government will arise among them out from their growth in life. Then we will be able to help them realize the governing power and the serving ability. The result will be a very proper government established in that local church. Thus, if we desire to have a sound government in a strong local church, we should stress the matter of the growth in life.

The New Testament confirms that the government of the church depends upon the growth in life. In the book of Acts there is very little mentioned concerning church government because Acts deals only with the beginning of the church when the saints were still young in the growth in life. In the Epistles from Romans to Revelation much more is mentioned concerning the government of the church. If we read these twenty-two books carefully, we will see that the government of the church is the outworking of the growth in life. For example, in Romans 8 Paul speaks concerning life. Those who experience this chapter have begun to mature in life and be conformed to the image of the firstborn Son of God (v. 29). Thus, after a parenthetical word in Romans 9 through 11, Paul begins to speak concerning the Body of Christ and the government of the church in Romans 12 through 16. Then in 1 Corinthians Paul deals with this matter further, revealing that there was something wrong with the government of the church in Corinth and indicating that this was due to a shortage of life (3:1-4). This is why in the first two chapters of this book the apostle tells the church in Corinth that they need the real experience of Christ as power and as wisdom (1:24). In these two chapters power refers to the power of life. The crucified and resurrected Christ as life is the power of the resurrection life and is wisdom to us. If we desire to have a strong local church with a sound government, we must experience the crucified and resurrected Christ. This is why Paul told the Corinthians that he had determined not to know anything but Christ and Him crucified (2:2). The Corinthians had power and gifts, but they did not have the proper government or a proper church because they lacked the experience of Christ.

The government of the church always goes together with the divine life. Apart from the divine life and the growth in this life, all we have is organization. We need life, and we need growth. Consider the example of the human body. When a child is only two months old, the members of his body are not sufficiently developed to function. Even when a child is two years old, his members are still not fully able to function. We cannot send a baby to school to attend the first grade. A baby can see and hear, but he is not mature enough to attend first grade. He must first grow and mature. If we could cause a baby to instantly become five years old, twenty-one years old, or fifty years old, it would be a miracle, but there are no such miracles related to the matter of life. In order to become twenty-one years old, a person must live for twenty-one years. For twenty-one years he must eat three meals a day and get a sufficient amount of sleep every night. With regard to life, there are no miracles; there are only principles. Not even modern science can cause people to mature more quickly. Since I have experienced and witnessed miracles, I believe in miracles. However, when it comes to the matter of life, there are no miracles. Time is required for the saints to grow in life. Thus, we need to help the Lord's children live, grow, and go on in a gradual way.

When it comes to the government of the church, nothing is more important than the growth in life. If the saints in a locality have the adequate growth in life, it will be easy for them to have the proper church government. If there is the growth in life among us, then spontaneously some brothers will begin to function in a certain way, and all the rest of the saints will recognize that these brothers are the elders. This is the way that a family governs itself. If all the members of a family gradually grow in life and are healthy, that family will spontaneously have a family government. Recently I observed the behavior of the children of a brother in whose home I was staying. I noticed that the oldest child took care of the younger children. When I saw him doing this, I knew that he was the oldest child. He was the "elder" among the children in that family. There was no need for the children to come together and vote to determine who was the elder among them. All the younger children automatically recognized that the oldest child was the elder among them. It was quite clear to them. It is the growth in life that makes this clear.

This principle applies to the deacons as well as to the elders in the church. Based upon their growth in life, some of the brothers and sisters will automatically rise up to serve the saints. Out of their love for the Lord, the church, and the saints, they will simply begin to serve. The Greek word for *deacon* means "a serving one." Thus, those who spontaneously begin to serve others based upon their growth in life are the real serving ones, the real deacons. When they begin to serve in this way, others will recognize that they are the deacons.

This principle also applies to all the ministries in the church. Perhaps one member of a family develops into a good cook, and another member of the family develops into a good sewer. Since these are their gifts, they will spontaneously take care of the cooking and the sewing in the family. This is also the case with the different ministries in the church. There is very little need for spending human effort to make arrangements. This is not to say that there is absolutely no need for any arranging but rather that this need is small. Similar to what takes place in a family, there is the need for only a small amount of arranging based upon what has already been expressed through the growth in life. We can do a little arranging based upon what has already been spontaneously expressed, but everything must be the outworking of the growth in life.

The Lord's way is the way of life and the growth in life. Thus, if we take this way, the Lord will honor it. This is truly wonderful, for when the Lord honors something, He blesses it. If, however, we take our own way, we will lose the Lord's presence, and there will be no blessing. When the Lord does not honor the way that we take, we are forced to do everything with our own human effort. Christianity has complicated the matter of the government of the church. In the denominations the government of the church is based almost entirely on organization. However, if we follow the Lord's way revealed in the Bible—the way of life—everything will be very simple, and we will receive the Lord's blessing.

A PROPER CHURCH NEEDING TO BE INCLUSIVE

Receiving Everything
That Is Scriptural and Spiritual

A proper church must not only take the way of life; it must also be inclusive. We must be inclusive of and open to all the Lord's children, and we must be inclusive of all spiritual matters. In particular, there are at least five items of which we must be inclusive—life, the truth, the church, the gospel, and power. In every local church we must have the line of the inner life, the line of the truth, the line of the church life, the line of the preaching of the gospel, which includes the preaching of the gospel in foreign countries, and the line of power, which includes the outpouring of the Holy Spirit and all the gifts of the Holy Spirit. A local church must be inclusive of these five lines. We should not say, "We are evangelical," or "We are solely taking the line of the church." Every local church must have a balanced diet. If we are not inclusive of these five lines, we will automatically become sectarian. I cannot agree with the fundamentalists who are against the Pentecostal movement. This is wrong. We must be inclusive of even the Pentecostal movement. Some other groups are opposed to the teachings of the Brethren, considering their teachings to be merely dead teachings. This is also sectarian and extreme. Although the Brethren may be lacking in life, many of their teachings are very sound. Thus, we must learn the truths that they teach. This does not mean that we should receive everything; we need to discern what is right and what is wrong. Nevertheless, we must be inclusive. If we are inclusive, the Lord will be with us. If we are exclusive, we will lose certain aspects of the Lord's blessing. We must receive, take, and be inclusive of everything that is scriptural and spiritual.

If someone comes among us and begins to speak in tongues, we must welcome him. If someone presents a certain truth from a passage of the Scriptures, we should receive him as well. This is the Lord's way. The Lord is deep and great, and what He gives to His Body is inclusive. Over the past two thousand years the Lord has given many things to His Body, and we must receive them all. However, we must not follow any one item to the exclusion of the others. We should receive every item, but we should not follow any one item in a particular way.

In the Far East, friends would often come to visit us. While they were with us, they would see many new things. After being with us for one day, they would say, "You people are very much like those in the Pentecostal movement." After being with us for a few more weeks, they would change their mind and say, "You people are very much like the Brethren." Then after attending another meeting, they would tell us, "Today you are just like the Methodists." After another month they might see a baptism among us, and then they would say, "Actually, you are just like the Baptists." In fact, all these observations are correct. This is why this part of the Lord's work in China has been so blessed by the Lord. It has been blessed because it is not closed to any of the Lord's children or to anything good that is from the Lord. We receive everything that is of the Lord. We have even received some things from the Catholics and have translated a number of books that were written by Brother Lawrence and Father Fenelon. Because we have been inclusive in this way, the Lord has blessed us.

Stressing Only Two Matters—
Christ and the Church

According to the Scriptures, we should stress only two matters—Christ and the church. If we are going to stress anything, we must stress Christ as life and everything to us and the church as the expression of Christ. These two items are all-inclusive; all the other items are contained within them. Many of us may have experienced some of the Pentecostal things, but we should never say that we are only Pentecostal. If we say this, we kill ourselves. The Pentecostal grace is only one of the many graces that the Lord has given and is still giving to His Body. Surely we must give heed to the experience of the baptism of the Holy Spirit, but we should not stress this too much. The experience of Pentecost is a minor point; it is not the central matter. The central matter is Christ and the church, that is, Christ with His Body. We agree with and appreciate all the good and scriptural things in Christianity, but if someone neglects Christ as life or opposes the church, we cannot stand with him. To neglect Christ as life or to oppose the church is to spoil the Lord's eternal purpose. Everything is for Christ and the church, including justification, sanctification, and the baptism of the Holy Spirit. Thus, we must be inclusive, but if anyone opposes Christ or is against the church, we cannot agree with him.

If we are genuinely inclusive of all the Lord's children and of all the good things that are of the Lord, we will be blessed by the Lord. On the one hand, we will be a reservoir to contain the Lord's blessing, and on the other hand, we will be a stream to flow out the Lord's blessing. Thus, let us all endeavor to be inclusive.

Learning to Be Inclusive
from the History of the Lord's Recovery

Martin Luther and Justification by Faith

If we consider the history of the church over the past four to five hundred years, we will see that during this time the Lord has recovered many things. The Lord's recovery began with the recovery of the truth of justification by faith. This truth was recovered through Martin Luther at the time of the Reformation. Following the Reformation, many other truths were recovered, including sanctification by faith, holiness by faith, the living of a life by faith, victory by faith, and many other items.

Count Zinzendorf
and the Initial Practice of the Church Life

In the 1700s some of the dear saints who were in the Lord's recovery began to pay attention to the church life. As a result, at that time in Europe there were many kinds of brethren meetings. In the eighteenth century some brothers moved to Bohemia to be with Count Zinzendorf. Under his leadership they began to practice the church life, and to some extent it was proper and even quite wonderful. At that time these saints experienced the baptism of the Holy Spirit, and this issued in a big revival. They enjoyed genuine brotherly love and truly practiced the church life. This was an all-inclusive expression of all the items that the Lord had recovered from Luther's time up to that point. These brothers received all the positive things that had been recovered before them.

The British Brethren
and Their Failure in Being Exclusive

The practice of the church life by the brothers in Bohemia was good, but the Lord desired to do something more. Thus, approximately one hundred years later, at the beginning of the nineteenth century, the Lord raised up some brothers in England under the leadership of John Nelson Darby. Their practice of the church life was even better than that of the brothers in Moravia. These brothers in England were very inclusive of all the positive things that the Lord had recovered before them. Unfortunately, they excluded anything further that the Lord tried to recover. They took in all the good things that had been recovered from the Reformation until 1828, but once they had received all those things, they felt satisfied and felt that what they had achieved was good enough. They did not realize that the Lord still had much more that He wanted to recover. As a result, they became exclusive and would not receive the things that the Lord recovered after them.

The Recovery of the Inner Life

After raising up the Brethren, the Lord continued to advance His recovery. The next major item that the Lord recovered was the inner life. For this the Lord used William Law and then Andrew Murray. Andrew Murray took all the good things that the mystics and William Law had recovered. Although Andrew Murray made great progress in the matter of the inner life, the Brethren excluded him and would not receive what he had recovered. Hannah Smith was also one whom the Lord used in recovering the matter of the inner life. She wrote the book *The Christian's Secret of a Happy Life* and was also excluded by the Brethren.

The Recovery of the Preaching of the Gospel

Outside the Brethren movement the Lord made great progress in the matter of the inner life. He also made improvements in the preaching of the gospel. Charles Spurgeon of England and D. L. Moody of America were both evangelical giants in the nineteenth century, but neither of them were in the Brethren movement. In fact, many of the missionaries who were sent to the mission fields and who spread the gospel over the whole earth were not part of the Brethren movement. Both the recovery of the inner life and the recovery of the preaching of the gospel were reactions to the Brethren movement.

The Pentecostal Movement

A third reaction to the Brethren movement was the Pentecostal movement. The Lord raised up the Pentecostal movement because the Brethren focused excessively on knowledge. The Brethren practiced the church life, but they were too much on the line of knowledge. Thus, the Lord responded by recovering the line of the inner life, the preaching of the gospel, and the power of Pentecost.

The Lord's Recovery in the Present Age— Inclusive of the Past and Open to the Future

In the present age the Lord desires to build up the church life and to bring in a new era of the church life. He is seeking after a people who will receive all the good things that have been recovered in the past and who are also open to the new things that He will do in the future. By the Lord's mercy and grace we have been practicing to take this way through the ministry of Watchman Nee for more than thirty-five years. This is why the Lord has blessed the work in China so much. When the Western missionaries came to China, we said to them, "Brothers and sisters, there is no need for you to come to China to build up different churches. Instead, you must join us and together we will build up the Lord's church in China. You do not need to come here to build up the Methodist church or the Presbyterian church; simply join with us." Although we spoke to them in this way, very few of them agreed with us. Nearly all of them wanted to keep their own "churches." As a result, they and their work received little blessing from the Lord. On the other hand, the work in China under the ministry of Watchman Nee has been prevailing. The reason it has been prevailing is that it is something according to the Lord's heart and the Lord's desire.

I believe that the Lord now wants to raise up something in the United States. Thus, if we are faithful to Him and take a stand to be inclusive of the past and open to the future, we will become a great reservoir to contain the Lord's blessing and a strong stream to flow the Lord's blessing to all the other countries throughout the whole earth. All that I have mentioned above is the history of the Lord's recovery, and we must learn from this history.

QUESTIONS AND ANSWERS

Question: What is the best place in which to hold the meetings of the church? Are the homes the best place?

Answer: From the Scriptures and from our experience, we have seen that there are two places in which we should have the meetings. The first place is in the homes. Without home meetings the saints will never have the opportunity to fellowship together in a thorough way. In addition to the homes, there is the need for a location where all the saints can come together to meet. This location can be either large or small. The book of Acts tells us that at times the saints in Jerusalem were separated into different meetings in their homes and that at other times all the saints assembled together (2:46; 12:12; 20:7-8).

Question: How often should the assembling of the whole church together take place?

Answer: This depends on the situation and the need. The whole church may assemble together weekly, bi-weekly, or monthly. At a minimum, all the saints should come together quarterly. The Scriptures reveal that the whole church should come together (1 Cor. 14:23, 26). There is definitely a need for this. In the church in Taipei this is our practice. At present we have thirty-seven district meetings in the church in Taipei during the week. On the Lord's Day the saints meet in nine different halls throughout the city. Then from time to time all the saints in Taipei will come together for a specific purpose— either to have some particular fellowship, to hear a message, or for a conference. Sometimes the whole church comes together to have the Lord's table. Most of the time, we have the Lord's table in the homes, less often we have the Lord's table in the nine halls, and periodically we have the Lord's table all together in one place. Sometimes several thousand attend this meeting.

Question: If there are thirty-seven district meetings, how do all of the saints know where they are supposed to meet?

Answer: All the saints know where they should go to meet because there is some church government. After a new convert has been baptized, the church assigns him to a certain district. This assignment is based upon where this new convert lives so that it is convenient for him to attend the meetings and for the church to take care of him. Once the saints in the church grow in life and the church government is arranged in a proper way, the handling of these kinds of practical matters becomes very easy. The only problem that we have in the church in Taipei is that we have too many new converts. We are like a family that has too many children and no one to take care of all of them. As a result, the brothers and sisters are hesitant to preach the gospel because they already have so many children. Those who are saved into the church respect the government of the church very much.

Question: Do you think that those who are saved respect the government of the church as a result of the way that people are

raised in the East? People in the West are very independent.
They do not like to be told what to do.

Answer: I do not think that this is the reason. In fact, I believe that the people in the West will respect the government of the church more than those in the East. The most important thing is that there is a proper government in the church. When there is a proper government, there will be the presence of the Lord, and everyone will respect the presence of the Lord.

When a proper government is raised up in a local church, the Lord honors it. Then if someone decides to rebel against the government of the church, the Lord's hand will come in. The Lord will take action in a clear way and deal with the situation. When some rebelled against Moses in the Old Testament, the Lord came in to vindicate Moses' authority (Num. 12:1-15; 16:1—17:13). Today, those who rebel against God's government will face a similar fate in that they will become spiritually dead.

Question: I am from a Presbyterian background. In the Presbyterian denomination all the pastors are hired. How do you find someone to preach the messages if you do not hire someone?

Answer: First, a proper church is like a home, a family. We all know how dear our home is to us. Second, a proper church is like a school where we can learn many things. The church takes care of our spiritual education. Third, a proper church is like a factory where we learn to work and manufacture and can practice what we have been taught. Fourth, a proper church is like a field where we learn how to farm. Fifth, the church is like a battlefield; we learn to fight the battle in the church. Sixth, a proper church is like a hospital, a place where all those who are sick can receive care. Thus, the church is all-inclusive. In such an all-inclusive environment, the members who are gifted will gradually be manifested and will begin to minister. After having been saved and having sought the Lord in a definite way in the church for eight to ten years, some will be manifested as having a ministry.

Question: Since it takes eight to ten years for a minister to be raised up, do you recommend that the church have an apostle or missionary during this time to care for the church?

Answer: This depends on the situation. In some places there may be the need for an apostle to stay for a period of time. In other places there may not be such a need.

Question: Would you say that it is necessary to have as a nucleus a few who see the proper way of the church?

Answer: Yes, this is necessary. We know that with anything, a good beginning is needed. If there is a good beginning, there can be a good continuation. In order for a local church to have a good beginning, there is a need for a nucleus of saints to stay in a certain place to lay a foundation. Once a foundation is laid, others will be able to follow more easily. We can see this in modern production processes. The most difficult matter in the manufacturing process is getting it started. However, once you have a factory in place and have begun production, it is easy to continue. Later, improvements can be made, but the key is to have a good beginning. As long as you have a good beginning, things will proceed automatically.

In the church life it is easy for some to be trained both practically and in life to become ministers for the Lord. When a new one comes into a proper church that has a proper government, after eight or so years this one, if he has a ministry, will be manifested as a minister. This is the right way to produce gifted ones. The right way to produce gifted ones is not through Bible institutes or seminaries; the right way is through the church. This is another reason why the church must be inclusive. The church must be inclusive so that all the new believers may be educated in many things. Those who come into the church in the Far East learn a great deal of the truth because we have many different studies in the church. Sometimes we study a book of the Bible, sometimes we study a particular topic, and at other times we study a special line of truth. In this way the new believers are able to receive a good spiritual education.

Question: Is the baptism of the Spirit an experience that a believer should particularly seek at the beginning of his Christian life, or is it something that a believer will experience without seeking?

Answer: The baptism of the Spirit is not an experience that is only for new believers. This experience is for all believers and is for our entire Christian life. We need to continually experience the baptism of the Holy Spirit.

The baptism of the Spirit is not a life matter but a matter related to power. This is seen very clearly in the life of the Lord Jesus. When the Lord was thirty years old, He came forth to serve the Lord, but before He began His service, He was baptized in water. Immediately following this baptism, the Holy Spirit descended upon Him as a dove (Matt. 3:16). This was the Lord's experience of the baptism of the Holy Spirit. For the first thirty years of His life before He received the baptism of the Holy Spirit, the Lord was surely living with God and before God. He was definitely One who was full of the divine life. We cannot say that prior to receiving the baptism of the Spirit, the Lord did not have the fullness of the divine life. The Lord surely had the divine life, but for His service He needed the Spirit to descend upon Him. This is a matter of power. Regrettably, many Christians today confuse these matters, thinking that the baptism of the Spirit is something related to life. Thus, they misunderstand this matter and misuse it.

CHAPTER FIVE

THREE NECESSITIES FOR OUR CHRISTIAN LIFE

Scripture Reading: John 3:6; 6:36, 57, 63; 15:4-5

BEING REGENERATED—JOHN 3

In John 3 the Lord met with a man named Nicodemus (vv. 1-13). Nicodemus, an elderly man, was an officer of the Jews. He was a teacher and was well educated, and he came to the Lord Jesus with the intention of obtaining some teachings. He considered the Lord to be one of the greatest teachers of all time, so he desired to obtain some of the best teachings and the best religion from the Lord. However, the Lord did not grant Nicodemus his desire. Instead, He revealed to Nicodemus that his need was not for teachings or even for the best religion but for life. The Lord said to Nicodemus, "That which is born of the flesh is flesh, and that which is born of the Spirit is spirit" (v. 6). The Lord's answer indicates that, apart from regeneration, flesh can never be changed into something other than flesh. Only by being born of the Spirit could Nicodemus be changed into something other than flesh, that is, into spirit. This points to our real need today. Our present need is not to receive some form of religion, knowledge, or teaching but to be regenerated by the Spirit of God. We need to be regenerated by God, with God, and through God to receive God Himself into us as life.

TAKING CHRIST AS OUR FOOD—JOHN 6

In John 6 the Lord performed a miracle by feeding more than five thousand people with only five barley loaves and two fish (vv. 1-13). As a result of this miracle the people who had been fed considered the Lord to be a great man and a great leader and wanted to make Him their king (v. 14-15). However, when these people came to the Lord the next day, the Lord, rather than likening Himself to a king or a great man, likened Himself to a small piece of bread. He told them that He was the bread of life that had come down out of heaven (vv. 33, 35). This indicates that the Lord came not to be a great leader but to be the life supply to His people. We do not need a great leader. Rather, we need the life supply; we need food. According to our concept, God is such a great God that when He became a man, He came as a great man. However, this was not the way the Lord came. He came down from heaven as the bread of life to be received by man and to be man's life supply.

In addition to telling His followers that He was the bread of life, the Lord said, "He who eats Me, he also shall live because of Me" (v. 57b). This indicates that the Lord is edible and that in order to live because of Him, we must eat Him. Every day we eat three meals, and it is these three meals that enable us to live. In other words, we live by what we eat. Thus, we need to consider what we eat and what the source of our living is. Do we live by the self? Do we live by knowledge, religion, teachings, or doctrine? We cannot live by these things. We must live by taking Jesus as our living food.

In Christianity there are many teachings. We must realize, however, that without the Lord Himself as the living One, neither Christianity nor its teachings profit us. Thus, our focus should not be Christianity or its teachings. Instead, our focus should be Christ Himself, the living One, as our food. Colossians 2:16-17 reveals that Christ is the body of all shadows. Food, drink, the Sabbath and the holy days, and the new moon are all shadows of which the reality is Christ. Since Christ is the reality, He Himself must be our focus. Day by day and moment by moment we must eat of Him as our real food and daily supply.

ABIDING IN CHRIST—JOHN 14 AND 15

In John 13:33 the Lord told His disciples that He was going to leave them. When the disciples heard this, they were very disappointed. They had been with the Lord for approximately three and a half years, and they treasured Him. They did not want to lose Him. Then the Lord told them that although He would leave them, He would return (14:3). He said that although He was going to leave them physically, He would return to be with them spiritually, that is, as the Spirit (vv. 16-18). Although the Lord was going to die, He would rise from the dead, and in His resurrection His body would be transfigured from a physical body into a spiritual body (1 Cor. 15:44). Furthermore, He would become the life-giving Spirit (v. 45). As the Spirit He would not only return to be with His disciples, He would also enter into them to dwell in them and to be one with them (John 14:20). After telling the disciples that He would return and enter into them as the Spirit, the Lord said to His disciples, "I am the vine; you are the branches" (15:5a). He told them that they would abide in Him and He would abide in them (v. 4). In saying this, the Lord assured them that He would never leave them because He would be in them, and they would be able to live with Him, in Him, and through Him. He also told them that by abiding in Him they would express Him (vv. 5, 8).

From these three portions of the Gospel of John—chapters three, six, and fourteen and fifteen—we see that our first need is to be regenerated by the Holy Spirit with Christ as life. We received our human life from our parents, but through regeneration we have received another life—the divine life. Because we have been regenerated, we must ask ourselves by which life we will live. Will we live by our natural life or by the divine life? Will we live by the self or by Christ? In Galatians 2:20 Paul tells us by which life he lived. He declares, "I am crucified with Christ; and it is no longer I who live, but it is Christ who lives in me." We must realize the spiritual fact that Christ is within us as our life and then learn how to deny our self, give up our natural life, and take Christ as our life (Matt. 16:24; Col. 3:4).

After receiving Christ as our life, our second need is to learn to feed on Christ day by day by contacting Him as the Spirit in our spirit. Just as a baby needs milk to feed on after it is born, we need to feed on Christ after we have been born of God with the life of God. Christ is not merely our life; He is everything to us. He is our life supply, our living food, and our living water. We need to feed on Him every day. It is not enough to go to the meetings of the church, to listen to messages, and to read the Word with our minds. We must learn to contact the Lord as the Spirit with our spirit. Whether we are reading, meditating, praying, or singing, we must exercise our spirit to contact the Lord as the Spirit. If we do this, we will be refreshed and satisfied.

About ten years ago I went to Manila. While I was there, I saw for the first time the drink called "7-Up." When I saw this name on the bottle, I wondered what it meant. After considering for a little while, I realized that the name "7-Up" probably means that if you drink this beverage, you will be uplifted and refreshed seven times. Then I thought to myself, "I do not need such a drink; I simply need more Christ. Christ is '700-Up.'" When you contact Christ even a little, you are refreshed and uplifted. When you are sitting in your office and are tired, you simply need to contact the Lord. Exercise your spirit and contact the Lord, telling Him, "Lord, I am tired." If you contact the Lord as the Spirit by exercising your spirit, you will be refreshed, satisfied, and strengthened by the Lord. Moreover, if you do this every day, day by day and moment by moment the Holy Spirit will gradually saturate you with all the riches of Christ until your whole being is filled with Christ. Your whole inner being—spirit, mind, emotion, will, conscience, and heart—will be saturated with Christ, making you a Christ-man. You will be full of Christ and will express Christ Himself.

In addition to receiving Christ as our life and learning to feed on Him as our daily food, our life supply, and our everything, we need to abide in Him. He is the vine, and we are the branches. As branches, we absorb all the goodness and riches of the vine. We absorb Him, live by Him, and are one with Him. First Corinthians 6:17 says, "He who is joined to the Lord is one spirit." We are one with Christ. He is living within us, and we are in Him. Our need today is to learn to abide in Him. We should never allow anything to separate us from the Lord. We must always remain in contact with Him. In this way He will be everything to us.

Being a Christian is not merely a matter of learning

teachings or trying to do good deeds. Being a Christian is a matter of being regenerated with Christ as life, feeding on Christ by contacting Him as the Spirit in our spirit, and abiding in Christ. If we do this, we will spontaneously bear fruit. Bearing fruit is not the result of human effort; it is the overflow of the life within, which is Christ Himself. As we abide in Him and allow Him to abide in us, He will fill us with Himself as life and will flow out of us as living water. As a result, we will bear much fruit. This is the real Christian life.

CHAPTER SIX

GOD'S INTENTION AND ITS ACCOMPLISHMENT

Scripture Reading: Rom. 8:9-10, 16; 1 Cor. 6:17; 2 Cor. 3:17-18; 4:16; Eph. 3:16-19; 4:22-24; Col. 3:9-11

GOD'S INTENTION BEING
TO WORK CHRIST INTO OUR BEING

God's eternal intention and purpose is to work Himself into us and to have Christ wrought into our being. This is not to make us good men but God-men. God's desire is to make us Christ-men—men who have been mingled with Christ to be one. There is nothing more important or basic in the whole universe than this matter. Why did God forgive, justify, cleanse, wash, sanctify, redeem, and regenerate us? He did all these things so that He could work Christ into us. Why do we wash the cups that we use for drinking? We wash them so that we can fill them with water. Similarly, God justified, redeemed, and regenerated us so that He could work Christ into us and cause us to be filled, saturated, and mingled with Christ. I fear that although many believers have been redeemed and regenerated and have even experienced the baptism of the Spirit, they do not know the purpose of God. The purpose of God is that Christ would be mingled with us so that we would be filled, possessed, and saturated with Christ and by Christ.

THE WAY GOD ACCOMPLISHES HIS INTENTION

By Creating Man as a Vessel to Contain God

The Bible reveals that man was created as a vessel to contain God. Second Corinthians 4:7 says, "We have this treasure in earthen vessels that the excellency of the power may be of God and not out of us." A vessel is different from an instrument. An instrument is a tool that can be used to accomplish some kind of work. A vessel is a container that is made to be filled with something. Man was not made to be God's instrument but to be God's vessel. We were made for the purpose of containing God. We are earthen vessels, and God Himself should be the treasure within us.

By Giving Man a Spiritual Organ to Receive Him

Since we were created to be vessels to contain God, we must ask how God comes into us and how we can receive Him. We do not receive God by thinking about Him with our mind or by touching Him with our hands. We receive God into us by means of our spiritual receiving organ. In God's wisdom, when He created man, He created man with many different organs to receive many different things. God created us with ears that we may receive music and sound. God created us with eyes that we may receive colors and images. God created us with a nose that we may receive air and odors, and God created us with a mouth and a stomach that we may receive food and drink. These are some of the physical organs that God has given us for receiving the things in the physical realm. God also created us with psychological organs for receiving the things in the psychological realm. For example, the organ for receiving thoughts is the mind. The eye is an organ for receiving something in the physical realm, and the mind is an organ for receiving something in the psychological realm, but what is the proper organ for receiving God, who is Spirit (John 4:24)? We cannot receive God with our eyes or with our mind; neither of these organs is the proper organ. Instead, deep within our being, in our innermost part, God created an organ for us to receive Him. This organ is our human spirit. This organ was specifically created for us to receive God. Just as God created us with a stomach for the specific purpose of receiving food, God created us also with a spiritual organ for the specific purpose of receiving God, who is Spirit.

Many would say that our spiritual receiving organ is our heart, but this is not the case. We can love God with our heart, but we cannot receive God with our heart. Our spiritual receiving organ is our spirit. Suppose I have a book that I would like to give to you as a gift, and suppose you like the book and even love the book. What organ would you use to love the book? Surely you would use your heart. However, you would not be able to receive the book with your heart. If I were to give the book to you, you would have to receive it with your hand. Once you received it with your hand, you could receive the information contained in it with your eyes and your mind. Regardless of how much you loved the book, you would not be able to receive the book with your heart. This is also the case with food. We all love to eat food. We may love food with our heart, but we cannot use our heart to receive food into us. To receive food into us we must use our hands, our mouth, and then our stomach. From these examples we can see that if we desire to receive something, we must use the right organ, and the right organ for receiving God into us is our human spirit.

John 4:24 says, "God is Spirit, and those who worship Him must worship in spirit." This verse clearly proves that we must receive God, who is Spirit, with our spirit. Romans 8:16 says, "The Spirit Himself witnesses with our spirit that we are children of God." The fact that the Spirit witnesses with our spirit proves that the Spirit has come into our spirit. First Corinthians 6:17 says, "But he who is joined to the Lord is one spirit." This verse points out that in addition to witnessing together, the Spirit of God and our spirit are joined together to be one spirit. The Spirit and our spirit are mingled together to such an extent that in Romans 8 it is difficult to determine when Paul is speaking concerning the divine Spirit and when he is speaking concerning our human spirit (vv. 4, 9).

By Becoming the Spirit in Our Spirit

Second Corinthians 3:17 says, "And the Lord is the Spirit; and where the Spirit of the Lord is, there is freedom." According to this verse the Lord Himself is the Spirit. John 1:14 tells us that the Word, Christ, became flesh. When Christ was on the earth before His death and resurrection, He was a man in the flesh. However, in His resurrection from the dead He was transfigured from the flesh to the Spirit (1 Cor. 15:45b). Today the Lord is the Spirit. Hence, when the Spirit comes into us, Christ Himself comes into us. This is not merely a doctrine or a teaching; this is a reality. Christ today is the Spirit dwelling within our spirit to be our life and everything.

Romans 8:9-10 shows us that both Christ and the Spirit are within us and that the two are actually one. These verses say, "But you are not in the flesh, but in the spirit, if indeed the Spirit of God dwells in you. Yet if anyone does not have the Spirit of Christ, he is not of Him. But if Christ is in you, though the body is dead because of sin, the spirit is life because of righteousness." From these verses we can see that the Spirit of God dwells within us, that we have the Spirit of Christ, and that Christ Himself is within us. Because the Spirit of God dwells in us, we have the Spirit of Christ. The Spirit of God and the Spirit of Christ are not two Spirits; rather, they are one. Thus, if the Spirit of God dwells in us, we also have the Spirit of Christ. Moreover, because we have the Spirit of Christ, we have Christ Himself within us. The Spirit of Christ is Christ Himself. God is triune; He is three-one. The Father is in the Son, and the Son is in the Father (John 14:10). Thus, if we have the Spirit dwelling within us, we also have the Son dwelling within us, and if we have the Son dwelling within us, we also have the Father dwelling within us.

THE WAY FOR US TO COOPERATE WITH GOD'S INTENTION

By Seeing That Christ Is within Us

Since God's eternal purpose is to work Himself into us, we need to see how we can be saturated with Christ and possessed by Him in a full way. We also need to see the way to experience Christ as our life in a practical way in our daily life. The way for us to experience Christ in such a way is very simple. Christ today is the Spirit (2 Cor. 3:17), we human beings have a human spirit (Job 32:8; 1 Cor. 2:11), and as the Spirit, Christ is dwelling within us in our spirit (2 Tim. 4:22). We do not need to ask Christ to come into us, because He is within us already. I recently heard a story about a man who was looking everywhere for his glasses because he had forgotten that he had put them on his head. Many Christians today are like this. Although they already have Christ within them, they are still looking for Christ. We all need to see that Christ is within us. He is the Spirit within our spirit. The fact that Christ is within our spirit cannot be a mere doctrine, teaching, or Christian slogan to us; it must be our fact and our reality.

Approximately thirty years ago the Lord opened my eyes, and I realized that the almighty, all-inclusive God is within me. When I had this realization, I was beside myself. I had to jump up and praise the Lord for being within me. At that time I felt that I was too big for the room in which I was. In fact, I felt that I was too big for the whole universe. It is a wonderful fact that Christ is in us, but many Christians do not know this. Second Corinthians 4:7 says, "We have this treasure in earthen vessels." Christ is the peerless treasure within us, who are the earthen vessels. We all must praise the Lord that He is within us and that because He is within us, we have the way to enjoy and experience Him. There is no need for us to go up to the heavens to bring Christ down (Rom. 10:6-8). Philippians 4:5b says, "The Lord is near." How near is the Lord? He is so near that He is mingled with us as one. Wherever we are, there He is. Because the Lord is so close to us, it is easy for us to experience Him.

By Putting Off the Old Man and
Putting On the New Man

To experience Christ in a full way, we also must learn to reject our old man. As those who have believed into the Lord and have received Him into us, we all have been born twice. Our first birth was of Adam through our parents; our second birth was of Christ through the Spirit (John 3:6). As a result of these two births, we have both an old man and a new man (Eph. 4:22-24). This is a rather complicated situation. Since we have been born again, we are of Christ, yet we still have the old man, and Adam is still with us. Often when I spend time with the Lord, I tell Him, "Lord, You know better than I do. Although You have regenerated me, You have still left the old man with me. Lord, I am not complaining, but dealing with the old man is a hard business for me. The old man is quite troublesome. What am I to do? I have been born again, and I have You as my new man and my new life, but as You know, I still have the old man." The Lord's intention in leaving us with the old man is that the old man, which is our outer man, would be consumed, and that the new man, which is our inner man, would be renewed (2 Cor. 4:16). When our inner man is renewed and we live in the new man, Christ becomes everything within us, because Christ is all and in all in the new man (Col. 3:9-11).

The way the Lord accomplishes the consuming of our outer man and the renewing of our inner man is twofold; He uses the environment, and He strengthens us into our inner man, our spirit. The Lord puts us into particular circumstances, and these circumstances work to consume our outer man. When the outer man has been consumed, the way is open for the inner man to be renewed. In addition to using particular circumstances to consume our outer man, the Lord also strengthens us into our inner man, the new man, where Christ is all and in all. We should not do anything to help our outer man, which is the old man. Instead, we should cooperate with the Lord's work and pray to the Father that He would strengthen us with power into our inner man (Eph. 3:14-16). When we are strengthened into our inner man, Christ makes His home in our hearts, and we are able to apprehend the immeasurable dimensions of Christ with all the saints (vv. 17-18). This is to experience Christ in an immeasurable way. We also will know the knowledge-surpassing love of Christ and will be filled unto all the fullness of God (v. 19). This experience is wonderful but also very basic. We all need to have such an inward experience of Christ. This is not to experience Christ outwardly as power but inwardly as life. This is God's intention.

Our old man is a troublesome person who constantly follows us. We must never go along with the old man. Rather, we must look down on him and consider him as our enemy. The key to experiencing Christ is to put off the old man and to put on the new man. Moment by moment we should learn to put off and put on. While we are dealing with our spouse or with our in-laws, we need to put off and put on. The old man is the self. Never agree with him, never respect him, and never go along with him. Instead, always go along with your inner man, which is Christ Himself, who is the Spirit.

Christians often speak of the cross, but the way to experience the cross in a practical way is to exercise our spirit to put off the self, to deny the self, and to turn our inner being to agree with the Spirit and to go along with the Spirit. If we do this, we will sense the presence and even the smile of Christ. By putting off the old man and putting on the new man, we will experience Christ as our life and everything, and Christ will possess, occupy, and saturate us. We will become people who are full of Christ and who are mingled with Christ as one. May the Lord help us to experience Christ in this way, and may we all pray to be strengthened into the inner man that we may deny the self and go along with the inner man so that we would be filled unto all the fullness of God. May we be fully saturated with the Triune God so that all that God is and has would be our portion. This will make us not merely good men but God-men.

God's eternal intention is to work Christ into our being. For the accomplishment of this intention, God created man as a vessel and gave man a spiritual organ to receive God Himself into him. Furthermore, Christ became the Spirit and entered into man's spirit. Since God's intention is to work Christ into our being, we must see the way for us to cooperate with this intention. The way for us to cooperate with God's intention is to see that Christ is living within us and to deny our old man, the self, and live in our new man. By our living in our new man, Christ will be able to work Himself into our entire being until He is all and in all in us. May the Lord bring us all into this experience.

CHAPTER SEVEN

TWO MYSTERIES IN THE SCRIPTURES— THE TRIUNE GOD AND THE RELATIONSHIP BETWEEN ETERNAL SALVATION AND GOD'S JUDGMENT OF HIS CHILDREN

THE TRIUNE BEING OF GOD

The Person of God Being a Mystery

The person of God is a mystery. It is far beyond our limited, human understanding. Thus, whenever we touch this matter, we need to be very careful and must avoid going into too much detail. In the second century the church fathers argued a great deal concerning this matter, and the things they argued about remain unresolved to this day. This is because the person of God is a mystery that is beyond the limits of our understanding. Whatever we say concerning this mysterious topic must be based upon two things—the revelation in the Scriptures and our experience. In addition to the Scriptures, we must consider our experience, but our experience must always be based upon the Scriptures and must never contradict the Scriptures.

The Revelation of the Scriptures concerning the Person of God

The first sentence of the Scriptures reveals that God is triune. Genesis 1:1 says, "In the beginning God created the heavens and the earth." In the original Hebrew text of this verse the word *God* is not singular but plural. In the Newberry Reference Bible Mr. Newberry put symbols next to certain words in the text of the King James Version to indicate the number, tense, or time of the corresponding words used in the original Hebrew text. Next to the word *God* in Genesis 1:1 he put three horizontal lines, indicating that the number of the Hebrew word for God is plural. This reveals that God has the aspect of three. This does not mean, however, that there are three Gods. This can be seen from the verb used in this verse. Although in this verse the subject *God* is plural in number, the verb *created* is not plural but singular. This is quite peculiar. Anyone who knows grammar knows that the subject and the verb of a sentence should match in number. If the subject is plural, the verb should also be plural. The fact that the subject *God* is plural and the verb *created* is singular reveals that God is triune or three-one.

In several other verses in Genesis God refers to Himself in the plural. Genesis 1:26 begins, "And God said, Let Us make man in Our image, according to Our likeness." In 3:22 God says, "Behold, the man has become like one of Us," and in 11:7 He says, "Come, let Us go down and there confound their language, that they may not understand one another's speech." In Isaiah 6:8 the Lord also refers to Himself in the plural when He asks, "Whom shall I send? Who will go for Us?" Do these verses mean that there is more than one God? Surely they do not, for other verses in the Bible clearly state that there is only one God. Isaiah 45:5 says, "I am Jehovah and there is no one else; / Besides Me there is no God." First Corinthians 8:4b states, "There is no God but one," and 1 Timothy 2:5a declares, "For there is one God." Although the Bible clearly reveals that there is one God, God Himself repeatedly refers to Himself in the plural number. This is a mystery that we cannot understand.

Isaiah 6:3 records the way in which the seraphim praised God in the Old Testament. They declared, "Holy, holy, holy, Jehovah of hosts." Revelation 4:8 describes the way in which the living creatures praise God in the New Testament. They proclaim, "Holy, holy, holy, Lord God the Almighty." Why is it that in both the Old Testament and the New Testament God is praised in the same way, and why is it that both the seraphim and the living creatures repeat the word *holy* three times? Would it not have been enough for them to say "holy" one time? Surely this is an indication of God's triune being.

In Numbers 6 the Lord spoke to Moses regarding the way in which Aaron and his sons were to bless the children of Israel. Verses 22-26 say, "Then Jehovah spoke to Moses, saying, Speak to Aaron and to his sons, saying, Thus you shall bless the children of Israel; you shall say to them, Jehovah bless you and keep you; Jehovah make His face shine upon you and be gracious to you; Jehovah lift up His countenance upon you and give you peace." Here again we have something that is done three times. This is a threefold blessing. The first part of this blessing is that Jehovah would bless the children of Israel and keep them. This refers to God the Father (Eph. 1:3; John 17:11, 15; 1 Pet. 1:5). The second part of this blessing is that Jehovah would make His face shine upon them and be gracious to them. This blessing speaks of light and grace, which are related to God the Son (Luke 1:78; Matt. 4:16; John 9:5; 1:14, 16-17). The third part of this blessing is that Jehovah would lift up His countenance upon them and give them peace. This refers to the Holy Spirit, who brings us the Lord's presence and gives us the peace of God (14:16-18; Phil. 4:7). Thus, the threefold blessing in this verse points to the Triune God.

The Lord's prayer in Matthew 6 also alludes to the Divine Trinity. At the opening of this prayer the Lord prays, "Our Father who is in the heavens, Your name be sanctified; Your kingdom come; Your will be done, as in heaven, so also on earth" (vv. 9-10). Here the Lord says the word *Your* three times. The first time—"Your name be sanctified"—refers to the Father. The second time—"Your kingdom come"—refers to the Son, for the Son is the King of the kingdom (Col. 1:13; Rev. 11:15; 19:16). The third time—"Your will be done"—refers to the Holy Spirit. Both the blessing in the Old Testament and the Lord's prayer in the New Testament are threefold.

The New Testament is filled with verses that highlight three aspects of the Triune God. Second Corinthians 13:14 says, "The grace of the Lord Jesus Christ and the love of God and the fellowship of the Holy Spirit be with you all." Matthew 28:19 reads, "Go therefore and disciple all the nations, baptizing them into the name of the Father and of the Son and of the Holy Spirit." In this verse the Greek word for name is singular, but the one name is shared by three. This is a mystery, revealing to us that God is triune.

Ephesians 1:3 also speaks of the Triune God, saying. "Blessed be the God and Father of our Lord Jesus Christ, who has blessed us with every spiritual blessing in the heavenlies in Christ." In the phrase *God and Father* we see God the Father; in the phrase *our Lord Jesus Christ* we see God the Son; and in the phrase *every spiritual blessing* we see God the Spirit. Here the three of the Trinity are clearly seen. Ephesians 3:14-17 further reveals the three of the Triune God. Verse 14 says, "For this cause I bow my knees unto the Father." This speaks of God the Father. Verse 16 continues, "That He would grant you, according to the riches of His glory, to be strengthened with power through His Spirit into the inner man." This verse speaks of God the Spirit. Then verse 17 says, "That Christ may make His home in your hearts through faith." Here we have God the Son. These three verses show the three of the Godhead working together.

The Bible reveals that God is three—the Father, the Son, and the Spirit—but this does not mean that there are three Gods. The Bible clearly states that God is one, and there are several verses that join the three of the Godhead together. For example, Isaiah 9:6 reveals that the Son is the Father. This verse says, "For a child is born to us, / A Son is given to us; / And the government / Is upon His shoulder; / And His name will be called / Wonderful Counselor, / Mighty God, / Eternal Father, / Prince of Peace." The child who is born is the Mighty God, and the Son who is given is the Eternal Father. The fact that the child is God and the Son is the Father is beyond our understanding. Some theologians attempt to explain this verse by saying that the Son is not the Father but is simply called the Father. The reason they put forth this explanation is that they believe that the Son and the Father are separate. This explanation, however, is not according to the Scriptures and is not reasonable. It would be unreasonable for people to call you Mr. Smith if you were not Mr. Smith. If people call you Mr. Smith, then you must be Mr. Smith. The Son is called the Father because the Son is the Father. John 14 also reveals that the Father and the Son are one. In verse 8 Philip asked the Lord to show them the Father. In verse 9 the Lord responded to Philip, "Have I been so long a time with you, and you have not known Me, Philip? He who has seen Me has seen the Father." The Lord's answer shows that He and the Father are one (10:30). While Isaiah 9:6 and John 14:8-9 reveal that the Son is the Father, 2 Corinthians 3:17 unveils that the Son is the Spirit. This verse begins, "And the Lord is the Spirit." The Son is the Father, and the Lord, who is the Son (4:5), is the Spirit. We may not be able to understand this, but we must accept it, for this is the revelation of the Scriptures.

Zechariah 2:10-11 is another mysterious passage. These verses say, "Give a ringing shout and rejoice, O daughter of Zion, for now I am coming, and I will dwell in your midst, declares Jehovah. And many nations will join themselves to Jehovah in that day and will become My people; and I will dwell in your midst, and you will know that Jehovah of hosts has sent Me to you." In these verses the One who will dwell in the midst of the children of Israel is Jehovah, but this One is also sent by Jehovah. He is sent by Jehovah, and He is Jehovah. How can this be? This matches the revelation of the rest of the Scriptures. In John 5 the Lord repeatedly declared that He had been sent by the Father (vv. 23, 30, 36-38), and in Isaiah 9:6 we see that the Son is the Father. The Son is sent by the Father, and the Son is the Father.

Romans 8:9-10 also shows us that we cannot divide the three of the Trinity. Verse 9 says, "But you are not in the flesh, but in the spirit, if indeed the Spirit of God dwells in you. Yet if anyone does not have the Spirit of Christ, he is not of Him." The Spirit of God dwelling in us equals our having the Spirit of Christ. This shows that the Spirit of God is the Spirit of Christ. Then verse 10 continues, "But if Christ is in you...." This proves that the Spirit of Christ is Christ Himself. The Spirit of God is the Spirit of Christ, and the Spirit of Christ is Christ Himself. This is the teaching of the Scriptures. No one can deny that God is three-one. Based upon this revelation, students of the Bible use the word *trinity*. Some would argue that the word *trinity* is not in the Scriptures. It is true that we cannot find such a word in the Bible, but we cannot deny the fact that such a thing exists.

Our Experience of God
Matching the Revelation of the Scriptures

Our experience also shows us that it is impossible to separate the Father from the Son or the Lord from the Spirit. According to 1 Corinthians 12:3, we may contact the Spirit by saying, "Jesus is Lord!", and according to Galatians 3:14 we may receive the Spirit by believing in Jesus. The One who comes into us is the Spirit, yet the One whom we believe in and call upon is the Lord Jesus. Calling "O Lord Jesus" also leads us to the Father. After praying to the Lord for a certain amount of time, we may find ourselves saying, "O Father in heaven." The more we say "Lord Jesus" and "O Father in heaven," the more we have peace and joy within. In our experience it is impossible to separate the Father from the Son or to separate the Son from the Spirit. This is because the Father, the Son, and the Spirit are truly one.

The Father Being the Source,
the Son Being the Expression, and the Spirit
Being the Fellowship of the Triune God

We can illustrate the triune nature of God with the three forms of water. If you leave a block of ice in the sun for an hour, it will become water. Then if you leave the water in the sun for half a day, the water will become vapor. Are the ice, water, and vapor three things or one thing? They are one thing in three stages, appearances, and forms. Ice is ice, water is water, and vapor is vapor, but in substance these three items are one. In appearance they are three, but in substance they are one. This is an illustration of the Triune God. In the Scriptures the Father is the source; He is like the block of ice. The Son, who is the expression of the Father, can be likened to the water. John 1:18 says, "No one has ever seen God; the only begotten Son, who is in the bosom of the Father, He has declared Him." The Father is the source, and the Son is His declaration, manifestation, and expression. The Spirit, which is the communion and fellowship of God to us, can be likened to the vapor (2 Cor. 13:14; John 20:22). Vapor is very easy for us to take in; all we need to do is breathe. Sometimes when the air in a room is too dry, we put a vaporizer in the room to moisturize the air so that as long as we are breathing, we are receiving the water into us. Through the Spirit, who is the communion and fellowship of God to us, we can receive God Himself into us.

THE RELATIONSHIP BETWEEN ETERNAL SALVATION AND GOD'S JUDGMENT OF HIS CHILDREN

Salvation Being a Free Gift and Being Eternal

Another mystery in the Scriptures is the relationship between eternal salvation and God's judgment of His children. The salvation of God is absolutely a matter of grace and has nothing to do with works. Ephesians 2:8-9 says, "For by grace you have been saved through faith, and this not of yourselves; it is the gift of God; not of works that no one should boast." Some have the concept that if we commit a sin after we have been saved, we will lose our salvation. This is not logical. If salvation is absolutely a matter of grace and has nothing to do with works, it is not logical to think that we can lose our salvation by doing something wrong. If it were possible for us to lose our salvation through wrongdoing, salvation would have something to do with works. Once we receive salvation, we can never lose it. In John 10:28 the Lord makes this matter very clear, saying, "And I give to them eternal life, and they shall by no means perish forever, and no one shall snatch them out of My hand." The life that we have received is eternal, and we can never perish (3:16).

First Corinthians 5:5 gives us an example of a brother who committed a terrible sin yet did not lose his salvation. Speaking of this brother, Paul says, "Deliver such a one to Satan for the destruction of his flesh, that his spirit may be saved in the day of the Lord." Although this brother had committed a serious sin, Paul says that he would still be saved in the day of the Lord. Once we are saved, we can never lose our salvation.

The Believers Receiving a Reward or Punishment
Based upon Their Life and Work
after They Are Saved

The Scriptures are clear that we can never lose our salvation, but how does God deal with believers who commit sins
and refuse to repent even after they have been saved? The
answer to this question is rather complicated. Our God is
wise, and He has many ways to deal with His people. First
Corinthians 3:13-15 shows us one of the ways that God deals
with His people after they have been saved. Verse 13 says,
"The work of each will become manifested; for the day will
declare it, because it is revealed by fire, and the fire itself will
prove each one's work, of what sort it is." This verse tells us
that when the Lord comes back, there will be a test to determine what sort of work we did after we were saved. Then
verse 14 continues, "If anyone's work which he has built upon
the foundation remains, he will receive a reward." This verse
speaks of a reward, not of salvation. Receiving a reward is different from receiving salvation. Verse 15 follows, "If anyone's
work is consumed, he will suffer loss, but he himself will be
saved, yet so as through fire." This verse says that if our work
is consumed, we will suffer loss. It does not say that we will
perish. Suffering loss is different from perishing. This is
proved by the phrase *but he himself will be saved.* We will
suffer loss if our work is consumed, but we will still be saved.
However, we should not say that all will be well, because
although the verse says that we will be saved, it concludes
with the phrase *yet so as through fire.*

We will never lose our salvation. Salvation is eternal, and
the work of Christ on the cross, upon which our salvation is
based, is eternal (Heb. 9:12). This matter is clear. However,
after we are saved, we need to live according to the will of God
and according to Christ. If we do this, we will receive a reward
when the Lord returns. This reward is something in addition
to salvation. However, if we do not live according to the will of
God and according to Christ, the Lord will cause us to suffer
loss when He returns. This suffering will be a form of punishment to us. Once we are saved, we are saved eternally. This

matter is settled once and for all. However, in addition to the question of salvation, there is the question of reward or loss. This is the clear teaching of the Scriptures.

All Believers Being Judged
at the Judgment Seat of Christ
When Christ Returns

The Bible reveals that there are several different kinds of judgments of God. Revelation 20:11-15 says that there will be a final judgment at the great white throne. This judgment has nothing to do with Christians. There is, however, another judgment spoken of in the Bible that does pertain to believers—the judgment at the judgment seat of Christ (Rom. 14:10; 1 Cor. 4:5; 2 Cor. 5:10). When Christ returns, He will set up His judgment seat, and all His disciples will be brought there to be judged. At this judgment seat only the saved ones will be judged. This judgment is not for eternal salvation or eternal destruction; rather, it is to determine who will receive a reward and who will suffer loss. If we have lived and worked according to the will of God, we will receive a reward. If we have not, we will suffer loss (Matt. 7:21-23; 25:1-30). This shows us the importance of how we live and work after we receive the Lord. We must be careful; otherwise, we will suffer loss.

The Apostle Paul Being One Who Lived
with a View to the Judgment Seat of Christ and
Who Endeavored to Obtain the Reward

The apostle Paul was one who lived with a view to the judgment seat of Christ and who endeavored to obtain the reward. In 1 Corinthians 9:25-27 he writes, "Everyone who contends exercises self-control in all things; they then, that they may receive a corruptible crown, but we, an incorruptible. I therefore run in this way, not as though without a clear aim; I box in this way, not as though beating the air; but I buffet my body and make it my slave, lest perhaps having preached to others, I myself may become disapproved." Clearly Paul had been saved, but in these verses he tells us that he was still running. Why was he running? He was running to obtain a prize, a reward. Paul even said that he was afraid that he might become disapproved. Does this mean that there was a possibility that Paul could lose his salvation? Surely it does not. Some versions of the Bible translate the phrase *become disapproved* as "be cast away." To be cast away does not mean to lose one's salvation; it means to be cast away from the prize.

Paul continues his thought in 10:1-5, saying, "For I do not want you to be ignorant, brothers, that all our fathers were under the cloud, and all passed through the sea; and all were baptized unto Moses in the cloud and in the sea; and all ate the same spiritual food, and all drank the same spiritual drink; for they drank of a spiritual rock which followed them, and the rock was Christ. But with most of them God was not well pleased, for they were strewn along in the wilderness." All the children of Israel were saved by the passover and crossed through the Red Sea, but not all of them entered into Canaan. On the one hand, they all were saved, but on the other hand, not all of them received the prize, the reward. In light of this warning, the apostle Paul tells us that he was running the race and striving to obtain the prize.

At the time Paul wrote the book of Philippians, he was still pressing on. In Philippians 3:13-14 he declares, "Brothers, I do not account of myself to have laid hold; but one thing I do: Forgetting the things which are behind and stretching forward to the things which are before, I pursue toward the goal for the prize to which God in Christ Jesus has called me upward." Even at this juncture he did not consider himself to have already attained. Thus, he continued to pursue, to run the race, and to press on. Not until the end of his life did Paul have the confidence to say that he had obtained the prize. Knowing that he would soon be martyred for the Lord's sake, Paul told Timothy, "I am already being poured out, and the time of my departure is at hand. I have fought the good fight; I have finished the course; I have kept the faith. Henceforth there is laid up for me the crown of righteousness, with which the Lord, the righteous Judge, will recompense me in that day, and not only me but also all those who have loved His appearing" (2 Tim. 4:6-8). Paul had been saved, but throughout the course of his Christian life he ran to obtain the prize, the crown. This crown is a reward and is something in addition to salvation. At the end of his life Paul knew that he had obtained the reward. Paul also told Timothy that this reward was not for himself alone but for all those who love the Lord's appearing and coming.

The Bible Teaching Both Eternal Security and the Responsibility of the Believers

At the moment we believe in the Lord, we receive salvation, and once we are saved, we can never lose our salvation. However, after we are saved, we must ask ourselves how we will run the race of the Christian life. The way we run this race will determine whether or not we will receive the crown as a prize. As we have seen, our running the race of the Christian life also includes the way we work. If we do not work properly, we will suffer loss when the Lord returns. We will be saved, yet so as through fire.

This understanding of the Scriptures solves the problem between the Calvinists and the Arminians. On the one hand, there is eternal security; on the other hand, there is the settlement of the Lord's righteousness. The Calvinists and the Arminians have been fighting for generations regarding this matter. The Calvinists insist that salvation is eternal and is based upon predestination. They are correct, but they neglect the other side—the side of responsibility. The Arminians emphasize the side of responsibility, but they neglect the side of eternal security. The Scriptures, however, are balanced. Salvation is eternal; hence, we are eternally secure. However, after we are saved, we must be responsible to the Lord concerning how we run the race of the Christian life. Those who run successfully will receive a reward, a prize; those who do not will suffer loss and will be punished. This balanced view of the Scriptures reconciles the two sides.

We can illustrate the relationship between salvation and reward with the experience of a father and his children. It is not uncommon for a father to tell his children that if they do well in school, they will receive a reward, but if they do not do well in school, they will be punished. If one of his children works hard and does well, the father may reward this child, but if one of the children does not do well, the father may punish this child. Although the father may punish the child who does not do well, this does not mean that this child is no longer one of the father's children. A son can never lose his sonship, but he can be punished. This punishment is a loss to him. We can apply this illustration to our status as children of God. All those who have believed in Christ are children of God (John 1:12-13), but there are regulations in God's family. If we go along with these regulations, when Christ returns, He will reward us, saying, "Well done. Come and rejoice with Me" (cf. Matt. 25:23). If we do not go along with these regulations, when He returns, He will punish us (v. 30). He would never reject us and say to us, "From now on I will no longer take you as My child." He loves us and has saved us, so He would never do this. He will, however, measure out some kind of punishment and cause us to suffer loss if we do not live according to His regulations. We must be clear that we have been saved eternally. However, we should not be altogether at peace, because we have some responsibility before our Father. This is the balanced revelation of the Bible concerning eternal salvation and God's judgment of His children.

CHAPTER EIGHT

THE GENUINE BUILDING UP AND RECOVERY OF THE CHURCH AS THE BODY OF CHRIST

GOD'S INTENTION TO HAVE THE CHURCH, THE BODY OF CHRIST

The Scriptures reveal that God's eternal purpose, His intention, is to express Himself through His Son, Christ, and through the church as the Body of Christ (John 1:18; Heb. 1:3; 1 Tim. 3:16). What God has done in the past, what He is doing in the present, and what He will do in the future are all for this goal—to gain a group of people who are saved and filled with Him to be the Body of Christ as the expression of God in Christ as the Spirit. This is God's heart's desire and the central matter in the Scriptures.

The book of Romans reveals to us the full gospel, which comprises everything in the counsel of God. The first matter that Romans deals with is the matter of our sins and God's condemnation. Then it deals with our justification, our redemption, our salvation, and our sanctification, that is, our deliverance from the nature of sin. The last point, unveiled in chapter twelve, is that all of the saved and sanctified ones are the many members of the one Body of Christ, the church (v. 5). However, most of the Lord's children neglect this matter. Most expositions of the book of Romans cover the first eight chapters, dealing with condemnation, justification, and sanctification, and neglect the teaching of the Body in chapter twelve.

The very last matter mentioned in the entire Scriptures is the holy city, the New Jerusalem, which is built with precious stones (Rev. 21:18a, 19-20). Thus, the Scriptures tell us that God's intention is to have not a pile of stones but a building and that we saved ones are living stones for the building

(Matt. 16:18; 1 Cor. 3:9; 1 Pet. 2:5). However, most Christians pay attention to the stones and forget that the stones are for the building. If we know God's intention and know the Word, we will realize that although there are groups of Christians all over the earth, most of these groups are like heaps of stones instead of something built up. In Christianity there is no spiritual building as the house of God.

This is due to the strategy of God's enemy. God's enemy will allow the Lord's children to do almost anything except to build up the genuine, living church. The enemy may allow the Lord's children to preach the gospel or to bring people to the Lord, but he will always fight against the building up of the church. This is where the battle is, and this is what the enemy attacks. He knows that this is a strategic point in the battle between him and God, because if God can gain the genuine, living church on the earth, He can accomplish His purpose.

BUILDING UP THE CHURCH
INSTEAD OF OUR OWN MINISTRY

In Ephesians 4 Paul says, "He Himself gave some as apostles and some as prophets and some as evangelists and some as shepherds and teachers, for the perfecting of the saints unto the work of the ministry, unto the building up of the Body of Christ" (vv. 11-12). The Lord has given the apostles, prophets, evangelists, and shepherds and teachers for the building up of the Body. However, what we see in the Christian world today is not the building but many gifted persons who are individual, spiritual giants. People exalt these gifted ones, the preachers and ministers, forgetting that they alone are not the building. Many Christians today are even seeking to be spiritual giants or something special in the Christian world. However, this is not the Lord's way to accomplish His purpose. The Lord's way is to use ordinary believers as stones for the building. Most physical buildings are formed not of one large piece of special material but of many ordinary pieces of material.

In the New Testament age, Peter, John, and Paul were great apostles, yet what they built up was not their own ministries but the local churches. The apostle John was the last of the great apostles and was very experienced, spiritual, and successful in his ministry. However, the Lord did not want to build him up; the Lord wanted to build up the local churches. In Revelation the apostle John portrayed each of the seven churches in Asia as a lampstand (1:11-12, 20). He did not say that the apostles were like lampstands; rather, he said that the local churches were the lampstands standing for the Lord's testimony. The testimony of the Lord is with the local churches because the local churches are the genuine expressions of the Body of Christ.

Our work in China and Taiwan during the past thirty years has been to build up the local churches, not to build up anyone's ministry. In the United States Brother Watchman Nee's ministry has become somewhat famous through his book *The Normal Christian Life,* but in Taiwan many of the saints do not know who he is. This proves that our goal is the building up of the church, not the building up of Watchman Nee's ministry. When I left Taiwan to live and work in the United States, there was no need for me to make arrangements before my departure, because the whole work in Taiwan was in the hands of the brothers, not in my hands. The more we worked in Taiwan, the more the church was in the brothers' hands, because we were building the church, not our own ministry. The same thing happened when I moved from Shanghai to Taiwan in 1949. I had been working in Shanghai for a period of time before the war, and the church had been blessed by the Lord. However, in 1949 I received a cable from Watchman Nee saying that I should leave immediately because the Communists were very close to occupying Shanghai. Two days after receiving the cable, I left Shanghai. I could leave in such a sudden way because the church was not in my hands but in the hands of the brothers. Our testimony is that we are building up the church, not any person's particular ministry.

Although most ministers today take the direction of building up their ministry, the right direction is to build up the local churches. We who are in the work are merely the Lord's co-workers in building up the church (1 Cor. 3:9), which is His house (1 Tim. 3:15). In other words, the church is not ours but

His, and the church is the house of the saints. When we work with the goal of building up the local churches, our work is prevailing because we bring all the saints into function. When the saints come to the meetings, they do not have the feeling that they are coming to someone else's church; rather, they feel that the church is theirs. On the other hand, if we build up our own ministry or keep the church in our own hands, we will at the very least hinder the building work. If we build up a church so that it is in our own hands, the saints will have the feeling that they are coming to our church, and this feeling will hinder them from taking up the responsibility to build.

This is what happened in China when the missionaries from the West went to China and began to build up their own denominational churches. Those who attended their churches felt like they had to help that particular missionary and honor him by going to his church. However, the feeling in the genuine church is different. The saints in the genuine churches are always grateful whenever the co-workers visit, but their feeling is that the church is theirs, not someone else's. They take the responsibility of building up the church and feel that the church is their home, their house, which they must care for. When a brother comes to help them, he does not take up the burden or responsibility of the church; he simply helps the saints build up their church.

THE IMPACT OF THE BODY

The Lord's mind, thought, intention, and heart are for the Body, the church, and the building up of the local churches in various places. If there are a few thousand believers in a locality built up together as one Body, they will have an impact, but even if there are only a few saints in a locality built up together, they will still have an impact. None of them may be famous or gifted; everyone may be ordinary, yet because they are fitted together, coordinated, and knit as a living Body, they will have an impact. My physical body does not consist of giant members but of small members built together. Nonetheless, my body has impact. It can speak, see, hear, eat, drink, dress, sing, and more. When the members of my body are one, there is an impact. On the other hand, if the members of my body were detached, the impact would be gone; there would be only a heap of bones. When we look at the present situation in Christianity, we see mainly a heap of bones (cf. Ezek. 37:1-2). Thus, there is a need for the genuine building among the Lord's children.

Every spiritual matter is related to the Body. If we have the genuine building, we have everything. When we are built up as the Body and go to preach the gospel, the Body preaches the gospel. This kind of preaching is prevailing and effective. However, the Lord's children today have no appetite for this matter. Instead, they are all seeking their personal interests, personal salvation, personal victory, and personal healing, blessing, and spirituality. Many Christians are offended when we talk to them about the matter of the church or the building because they have no heart or appetite for this matter.

There are some seeking ones, however, who feel a need in their spirit and heart. These seeking ones long and seek for something more. They feel a need, but they do not know what they need and cannot explain what they are seeking. They have a thirst and a lack, but they cannot explain what will satisfy them. Though they may be very spiritual, they cannot be satisfied apart from the genuine church, the genuine building up of the Body. However, once they see the building of the church and enter into it, they feel satisfied and realize that this is what they were seeking. Their inner sense confirms this matter in them.

THE RECOVERY OF THE CHURCH

We have many items of truth and practice in the Lord's recovery, but we do not stress any of those items as much as we stress Christ and the church. We must experience Christ as our life and our everything, and we must have the church as the expression of Christ. If we stress these two matters, all the other matters will be resolved spontaneously and automatically. Many problems can be solved by helping people to experience Christ as their life and as everything in their daily living and by helping them to come together, submit to one another, and be built up together for the expression of Christ.

As long as we have these two items of Christ and the church, all other problems will be automatically solved.

Since the time of the Reformation about five hundred years ago, the Lord has recovered many items, and we feel that the building up of the church may be the last item of the Lord's recovery before He comes back. Before the Lord comes back, He must have the church on this earth. In the Old Testament when Absalom drove his father David away from Jerusalem, some people prepared the way for David to return. Similarly, there is the need for some prevailing churches on the earth to prepare the way for the Lord to come back. This will not be accomplished by Christianity as a whole. Rather, there needs to be a remnant—the New Testament overcomers. In the seven epistles to the seven churches in Revelation 2 and 3, the Lord sounds the call for the overcomers, the remnant (2:7, 11, 17, 26-28; 3:5, 12, 20-21). We believe that in the last days before the Lord comes back, He will send out a call for the remnant, the overcomers, to be built up together as the living expression of the Lord's Body. This will prepare the way for the Lord to return.

QUESTIONS AND ANSWERS

Question: Many Christians whom we contact come to the recovery for the blessings but simultaneously remain in their own denominations. When they need the Lord, they come here, but their money, work, and effort go to their particular denominations. It seems that they are interested only in taking away from the church and not in building up the church. How can we change this?

Answer: The Lord will not bless us if our intention is to pull people out from the denominations to help us. Our intention should be to help all the Lord's children. While we are working with such an intention, the Lord may sovereignly cause some brothers and sisters to come together to be a nucleus and to stand on the right ground and position to practice the real expression of the Lord's Body. As more blessing and more of the Lord's presence is realized, people will come to get the help. After they have been helped, they may go back to their denominations to help others. If this happens, we must let them go and believe that this is something under the Lord's hand. We must give them the full liberty to either remain in our meetings or return to their denominations. For the most part, we should not tell people to leave their denominations. We must believe that the Lord will sovereignly cause some saints to be clear concerning the recovery and that He will cause some to be a nucleus to bring in the Lord's blessing for His children.

Question: Could you give us an example from your experience of how a church is raised up and established?

Answer: Most of the local churches in China were raised up not through famous ministers or preachers but through the believers, those who had secular jobs in the world. For instance, perhaps a brother who is a schoolteacher is transferred to another city. When he arrives there, he begins to preach the gospel and to contact believers and have fellowship with them. This schoolteacher may invite his colleagues from school, his neighbors, or even his students to his home for a meal and some fellowship. In this way some may be saved, and these may lead others to be saved in the same way. Then these saved ones may begin meeting in the schoolteacher's home, and when the number of those meeting increases to a proper number, they may establish a local meeting. This way is very simple and effective. The local ones must preach the gospel.

In order to carry out the building up of the local expression of the Lord's Body, we must realize that the building must be started in the way of life, not in the way of a movement. The way of a movement does not work; only the way of life works. It is good and even necessary to pay attention to other experiences such as the experience of the baptism of the Holy Spirit. However, the most important thing is to help people to know Christ in the way of life. I am not against the baptism of the Holy Spirit, but the most vital factor for the building up of the church is life. All the experiences such as the baptism of the Holy Spirit and speaking in tongues are for the building up of the church, but the main factor is life. With our physical body, the most vital factor is life. Our bodies need exercise, air, and sunshine, but these things, though they are for life, are not life itself. Thus, in order to build up the church as the Body of Christ, we must help people to know Christ as life.

CHAPTER NINE

PUTTING ON THE CHURCH LIFE
TO HAVE THE REAL CHRISTIAN WALK

Scripture Reading: Eph. 1:22-23; 5:31-32; 2:14, 12, 15; 4:24

THE CHURCH BEING THE FULLNESS OF CHRIST

Ephesians 1:22-23 says, "He subjected all things under His feet and gave Him to be Head over all things to the church, which is His Body, the fullness of the One who fills all in all." These verses tell us that the Body of Christ is the fullness of Christ. What is the fullness of Christ? It is important to answer this question because in order to fully understand what the church is, we must understand what it means for the church to be the fullness of Christ.

Ephesians 5 gives us a key to understand what it means for the church to be the fullness of Christ. This chapter reveals that the church is to Christ what Eve was to Adam. After God made Adam, He took a rib out of Adam's side and built that rib into a woman, Eve (Gen. 2:21-22). Eve was a part of Adam, something that had come out of Adam; hence, she was Adam's counterpart, Adam's wife, and Adam's fullness. Previously Adam had been alone and had had no fullness, but when Eve was built from one of his ribs and was given to him to be his counterpart, she became his fullness. Just as Eve was the fullness of Adam, so also the church is the fullness of Christ. In order to take a rib out of Adam, God caused Adam to fall into a deep sleep. Similarly, in order for the church to be produced out of Christ, Christ died on the cross. When Christ was on the cross, His side was pierced, and blood and water flowed out of Him (John 19:34). The blood was for redemption, and the water was for imparting Christ's resurrection life into His believers to produce the church. Thus, out of the blood and water, the church was produced. The church is a part of Christ and is Christ Himself. The rib taken from Adam's side was the material for building Eve; likewise, the resurrection life that flowed out of Christ on the cross was the material for the producing of the church. Eve came out of Adam and was a part of Adam; the church came out of Christ and is also a part of Christ. Eve was given back to Adam to be his counterpart; the church will eventually become Christ's eternal counterpart (Eph. 5:27; Rev. 21:9-10). In all these ways the church today is the fullness of Christ.

THE CHURCH BEING THE BODY OF CHRIST

In addition to being the fullness of Christ, the church is also Christ's Body (Eph. 1:22-23). Christ is the Head, and the church is the Body. Actually, the Head is Christ, and the Body is also Christ. My head is me, and my body is also me. No one would ever say that his body is not himself. The Head Christ and the Body Christ form the universal Christ. It is a great revelation to see that the church, the Body of Christ, is entirely out of Christ.

THE CHURCH BEING THE NEW MAN

The church is also the new man. Ephesians 2:15 says, "Abolishing in His flesh the law of the commandments in ordinances, that He might create the two in Himself into one new man, so making peace." The two parties spoken of in this verse are the Jews and the Gentiles. Out of these two parties the Lord chose many people, and with these chosen ones He created the new man. The new man is the church, the Body of Christ (v. 16). Many Christians think that the new man is something individual, but the Scriptures reveal that the new man is corporate. The new man is a corporate body. In the whole universe there is only one new man; there are not many new men. This one new man is the Body of Christ, the fullness of Christ.

PUTTING ON THE CHURCH AS THE NEW MAN

The real Christian walk is a walk in the church life. This is why Ephesians 4:22 and 24 tell us to put off the old man and put on the new man. We have already seen that the church is the new man. Thus, to put on the new man is to put on the church, the Body of Christ. We seek to be victorious, but we must realize that the victorious life is the church life. If we put on the church life, which is the new man, everything will become easy for us. Whatever we try to do on our own is difficult, but whatever we do in the church life is easy. For example, often when we pray by ourselves to overcome a certain matter, it is very difficult for us to break through. However, when we bring the matter to the brothers and ask them to pray with us, we often break through after a single session of prayer. Suppose you are a person who easily loses his temper. If you try to deal with this matter by yourself, you may try for many years and still be unable to overcome it. If, however, you bring this matter to the brothers, open to them, confess to them that you have this weakness, and ask them to pray with you and to bear your weakness, you will get through. We should never keep things in our own hands; rather, we should bring everything to the Body. This is the practical way to put on the new man, and this is the real Christian walk.

The principle of putting on the church life also applies to spiritual experiences. Suppose you desire to experience the baptism of the Holy Spirit. If you seek this experience on your own, it will be difficult for you to obtain it. However, if you seek the baptism of the Holy Spirit together with the brothers in the church, it will be easy for you to obtain this experience. We all need to see that we are a part of the church, which is the fullness of Christ, the Body of Christ, and the new man. Since we are a part of the church, the new man, we must put on the new man by entering into the real church life.

The church is the fullness of Christ, the Body of Christ, and the new man. The church being the fullness of Christ means that the church is something of Christ and something that issues out of the resurrection life of Christ; the church being the Body of Christ means that the church is Christ Himself; and the church being the new man means that the church is a new creation (2 Cor. 5:17; Gal. 6:15). In addition to seeing all these aspects of the church, we must see that we are part of the church and that we must live the church life. In order to have the genuine Christian life and walk, we must put away the self, the old man, and put on the new man, which means that we must put on the church life.

If we have the real church life, we are truly living in the new man. If we have the real church life, we are truly spiritual. If we want to know how spiritual we are, we must consider how much we are in the church. How much do we live and walk in the church? How much of our being, our life, our walk, and our daily living are in the church? The church is the real test. If we put on the new man by living in the church life, we will enjoy and experience Christ in a full way. We all must live by Christ and live in the church. We all must have a Christian life and a church life. If we have both, we will experience Christ in a full way.

Chapter Ten

DISCERNING OUR SPIRIT
AND KNOWING THE DIFFERENCE
BETWEEN OUR SPIRIT AND
THE OTHER INWARD PARTS OF OUR BEING

Scripture Reading: Ezek. 36:26-27; Heb. 4:12; Mark 12:30; 1 Thes. 5:23; Heb. 10:22; Matt. 9:4; John 16:22; Rom. 10:1; Acts 11:23

OUR NEED TO DISCERN OUR SPIRIT

Second Corinthians 3:17 states that the Lord is the Spirit, Romans 8:16 reveals that the Spirit witnesses with our spirit, and 1 Corinthians 6:17 says that he who is joined to the Lord is one spirit. These verses reveal that the Lord who is the Spirit is living, dwelling, working, moving, and acting in our spirit. They also show us that if we desire to know the Lord in a practical way and to experience Him in our daily life, we must learn to discern our spirit. If we do not know our human spirit, we cannot understand God's moving within us and cannot follow the Lord, because the Lord today is the Spirit living within our spirit.

MAN HAVING MANY INWARD PARTS
AND ONE HIDDEN PART

If we have followed the Lord for some time, we may know in a general way that the Lord is within us, but we may not know exactly where the Lord is within us. Human beings are composed of many parts. Psalm 51:6 says, "Behold, You delight in truth in the inward parts; / And in the hidden part You would make known wisdom to me." This verse speaks of inward parts (plural) and a hidden part (singular). God desires truth

in the inward parts, and in the hidden part He causes us to
know wisdom. What are the inward parts, and what is the
hidden part? As Christians we need to understand these
matters.

KNOWING THE DIFFERENCE BETWEEN OUR SPIRIT AND OUR OTHER INWARD PARTS

Human beings have many inward parts. These parts
include the spirit, the soul, the heart, the mind, the emotion,
the will, and the conscience. We may be very clear about the
outward parts of our physical body, but we may not know
much about our inward parts. The Scriptures tell us that the
Lord is in our spirit (2 Tim. 4:22). Thus, it is very important
for us to discern our spirit and to realize that our spirit is
different from our soul, heart, mind, emotion, and will. We
may be clear that our spirit and our body are different, but we
must also be clear that our spirit is different from the other
inward parts of our being.

The Difference between Our Spirit and Our Heart

Ezekiel 36:26 helps us to see that our heart and our spirit
are not the same. This verse begins, "I will also give you a new
heart, and a new spirit I will put within you." In this verse the
Lord gives us a new heart and also puts a new spirit within
us. This shows that the heart and the spirit are two different
things. To understand the difference between these two, we
need to know the function of the heart and the function of the
spirit. Mark 12:30 reveals that the function of the heart is
to love the Lord. This verse begins with the charge, "You shall
love the Lord your God from your whole heart." Second Timothy 4:22 and John 4:24 reveal that the function of the spirit is
to receive and contact the Lord. Second Timothy 4:22 says,
"The Lord be with your spirit," and John 4:24 says, "God is
Spirit, and those who worship Him must worship in spirit
and truthfulness."

We often say that we love the Lord or that we have fellowship with the Lord. We must be clear, however, which part of
our being we use to do these things. For example, suppose you
love a certain book very much. You may love the book with

your heart, but you cannot take and receive the book with your heart. If you wish to take the book, you must use your hand. With regard to a book, the heart is the loving organ and the hand is the receiving organ. Just as our heart is the organ that we use to love a book, our heart is also the organ that we use to love the Lord. We love the Lord with our heart, but we cannot receive the Lord with our heart. Rather, we receive the Lord with our spirit. At the time of our regeneration, the Lord created a new heart and a new spirit within us. He gave us a new heart so that we could love Him, and He put a new spirit within us so that we could receive Him into us. Many Christians believe that as long as we love the Lord, we will be spiritual people. To them all that matters is the heart. This is wrong, because, as we have seen, we cannot receive the Lord with our heart. With our heart we can love the Lord, but if we desire to receive and contact the Lord and to have fellowship with Him, we must learn how to discern and exercise our spirit.

The Parts of the Heart

The Scriptures reveal that the heart is composed of four parts—the conscience, the mind, the emotion, and the will. Hebrews 10:22 says, "Let us come forward to the Holy of Holies with a true heart in full assurance of faith, having our hearts sprinkled from an evil conscience and having our bodies washed with pure water." This verse shows us that the conscience is part of the heart, because the verse says that our heart can be sprinkled from an evil conscience. Matthew 9:4 says, "Jesus, knowing their thoughts, said, Why are you thinking evil things in your hearts?" This verse tells us that the heart can think evil thoughts. This reveals that the mind, our thinking organ, is part of the heart. John 16:22 says that our heart can rejoice, and Romans 10:1 states that pleasure is related to our heart. These two verses reveal that the emotion is part of the heart. Finally, Hebrews 4:12 makes it clear that the will is a part of the heart. This verse says that the Word of God is able to discern the thoughts and intentions of the heart. Intentions are something of the will. Thus, we can see that the heart is composed of the conscience, the mind, the emotion, and the will. The sum of these four parts is the heart.

Denying Our Mind, Emotion, and Will and Following Our Spirit

The mind, emotion, and will, which are all parts of the heart, are also the three parts that make up the soul, that is, the natural life, the self. These three parts are not parts of the spirit. Thus, if we desire to know the Lord and to follow Him, we should not endeavor to do so according to our mind, emotion, or will. If we are following our mind, emotion, or will, this indicates that we are not following the Lord, because the Lord is not in these parts but in our spirit. Often we think so much that we quench our spirit. At other times we do things that are against the Lord because we are so strong in our will. Moreover, we often find ourselves under the influence of our emotion, and this causes us to go against the Lord. This shows us that if we want to follow the Lord, we must deny our mind, emotion, and will. We must deny all these parts of our inner being and follow the spirit. When we follow the spirit, we follow the Lord Himself, because the Lord is in our spirit. He is not in our mind, emotion, or will but in our spirit.

Denying Our Mind

The Lord is in our spirit. Hence, it is critical for us to learn to discern our spirit and to know the difference between our spirit and our mind, emotion, and will. If we do not know this difference, we will often find our fellowship with the Lord frustrated. For example, many times while we are praying, we sense the presence of the Lord and have genuine fellowship with Him in spirit. Often, however, while we are having such fellowship, we suddenly exercise our mind and begin to think about or remember something. When we do this, immediately our fellowship with the Lord stops. Our fellowship with the Lord is hindered by our thinking and our mind. Our mind is often a source of trouble to us. Perhaps our mind is bothered by a certain brother. In our mind we are not happy with this brother, and the more we think about him, the more we want to give him up. However, while our mind is thinking about giving him up, we have an entirely different sense in our spirit. In our innermost part we have the feeling that we must love this brother. At such a time we need to decide whether we will follow our mind or our spirit. To follow the mind is to follow the self; to follow the spirit is to follow the Lord. In such a situation we must give up the self and tell the Lord, "Lord, I do not agree with my mind; I agree with my spirit. I reject my mind, and I take my spirit." This experience illustrates a basic principle—the way to follow the Lord is to do things not according to our mind with its thoughts but according to the inner sense and the deep consciousness in the innermost part of our being. We need to follow this deep inner sense because it is the sense of the Lord in our spirit.

Denying Our Emotion

If we desire to follow the Lord, we must deny our emotion in addition to denying our mind with its thoughts. Once a sister who was a co-worker came to me and said, "Brother Lee, I simply do not like the sister who is working together with me." This sister had a problem with her emotion. According to the feeling in her emotion, she did not like her sister. After this sister told me her situation, I said to her, "Sister, although you may not like your fellow sister, what is your sense in your innermost part?" When I asked her this question, tears began to roll down her face, and she said, "To be honest, in my innermost part I have the feeling that I must work with this sister and that I must love her." Then I asked her, "What are you going to follow? Are you going to go along with your own desire in your emotion, or are you going to go along with your innermost part, your spirit?" She answered me, "I know that I must go along with my spirit, but I do not want to do this." Then I told her, "Please do not tell this to me; tell it to the Lord. Tell the Lord that although you know that you must follow your spirit, you do not want to." After hearing my answer, the sister replied, "Brother Lee, I do not want to go to the Lord because I already know what He will say." Then I answered by telling her, "Sister, you must go to the Lord. If you do not go to Him today, you will have to go to Him tomorrow, and if you do not go to Him in this age, you will have to go to Him in the next. Eventually, you will have to meet the Lord. You have come to me, but I cannot help you. If you go to the Lord, the Lord will be able to help you. You must go to the Lord." This story applies to all of us. When we are troubled in our emotion, we must not follow our emotion; we must follow our spirit. If we do not want to follow our spirit, we must go to the Lord and open to Him. If we go to the Lord, the Lord will strengthen us to follow Him in our spirit (Phil. 2:13).

Denying Our Will

Sisters are often troubled by their emotion, but brothers are more often troubled by their will. Many brothers have a strong will; once they make a decision, they cannot change it. I once had a co-worker who had a very strong will. Once he had made a decision, no one could change him. One time he made the decision to go to a certain place to work, even though we all felt that it was not the Lord's will for him to do so. We told him how we all felt, but he gave us reason after reason why he had decided to go. Faced with his strong will, we had no choice but to send him. However, on the day that this brother intended to move to this new place, the Lord met him. He tried numerous times to leave, but each time the Lord intervened and prevented him from leaving. After his third attempt, I asked this brother, "Brother, how do you feel in your spirit?" I did not want to know how he felt in his mind or in his will but in his spirit. This brother answered, "Last night I was clear in my innermost part that I should not go." When he gave me this answer, I realized how strong his will was. He was so strong in his will that even when he was clear in his spirit that the Lord's will was against his own will, he still could not change his will. We need to realize that if we are going to follow the Lord, we cannot be this way. We must be simple and must deny our mind, emotion, and will in order to follow the feeling in the deepest part of our being. This is where the Lord is. The more we follow our inner consciousness and our deepest feeling, the more we will sense the presence of the Lord, enjoy the Lord, and experience the Lord.

The Result of Following Our Spirit

When we go along with our spirit and follow the sense in our spirit, there will be a result—Christ will make His home in our heart. Ephesians 3:16-17 says, "That He would grant you, according to the riches of His glory, to be strengthened with power through His Spirit into the inner man, that Christ may make His home in your hearts through faith." The Lord is dwelling in our spirit. When we go along with Him, the Father strengthens our spirit by His Spirit. This opens the way for the Lord to make His home in our heart and in our entire inner being. This means that the Lord fills our mind, emotion, will, and conscience. This is the Lord's desire, and this is the right way for us to experience the Lord. We may know that we need to be filled with the Lord and transformed into His image, but how can this take place? The way is for us to realize that the Lord as the Spirit is living, dwelling, and working in our spirit, to see that our spirit is different from our mind, emotion, will, and heart, and to give up what is not the spirit and follow the sense in our spirit. If we go along with our spirit, our spirit will be strengthened by the Spirit, and the result will be that Christ will make home in our hearts and fill all our inward parts with Himself. Then Christ will be everything within us, and our whole being will be filled with Christ. This is the way to follow the Lord and to live the genuine Christian life.

ABOUT THE AUTHOR

Witness Lee was born in 1905 in northern China and raised in a Christian family. At age 19 he was fully captured for Christ and immediately consecrated himself to preach the gospel for the rest of his life. Early in his service, he met Watchman Nee, a renowned preacher, teacher, and writer. Witness Lee labored together with Watchman Nee under his direction. In 1934 Watchman Nee entrusted Witness Lee with the responsibility for his publication operation, called the Shanghai Gospel Bookroom.

Prior to the Communist takeover in 1949, Witness Lee was sent by Watchman Nee and his other co-workers to Taiwan to ensure that the things delivered to them by the Lord would not be lost. Watchman Nee instructed Witness Lee to continue the former's publishing operation abroad as the Taiwan Gospel Bookroom, which has been publicly recognized as the publisher of Watchman Nee's works outside China. Witness Lee's work in Taiwan manifested the Lord's abundant blessing. From a mere 350 believers, newly fled from the mainland, the churches in Taiwan grew to 20,000 in five years.

In 1962 Witness Lee felt led of the Lord to come to the United States, settling in California. During his 35 years of service in the U.S., he ministered in weekly meetings and weekend conferences, delivering several thousand spoken messages. Much of his speaking has since been published as over 400 titles. Many of these have been translated into over fourteen languages. He gave his last public conference in February 1997 at the age of 91.

He leaves behind a prolific presentation of the truth in the Bible. His major work, *Life-study of the Bible,* comprises over 25,000 pages of commentary on every book of the Bible from the perspective of the believers' enjoyment and experience of God's divine life in Christ through the Holy Spirit. Witness Lee was the chief editor of a new translation of the New Testament into Chinese called the Recovery Version and directed the translation of the same into English. The Recovery Version also appears in a number of other languages. He provided an extensive body of footnotes, outlines, and spiritual cross references. A radio broadcast of his messages can be heard on Christian radio stations in the United States. In 1965 Witness Lee founded Living Stream Ministry, a non-profit corporation, located in Anaheim, California, which officially presents his and Watchman Nee's ministry.

Witness Lee's ministry emphasizes the experience of Christ as life and the practical oneness of the believers as the Body of Christ. Stressing the importance of attending to both these matters, he led the churches under his care to grow in Christian life and function. He was unbending in his conviction that God's goal is not narrow sectarianism but the Body of Christ. In time, believers began to meet simply as the church in their localities in response to this conviction. In recent years a number of new churches have been raised up in Russia and in many eastern European countries.